PEPE NUMMI

THE HANDBOOK OF FACILITATIVE LEADERSHIP

CONCRETE WAYS TO BOOST PERFORMANCE

Grape People

ISBN 978-952-69073-0-7 (nid.)
ISBN 978-952-69073-1-4 (EPUB)

Drawings: Oona Loman, Encore Digital Marketing Oy
and Agenda Helsinki Oy
Layout: Taru Tarvainen

Printed by CreateSpace

TABLE OF CONTENTS

FOREWORD

Pepe Nummi has been my guru when it comes to facilitative leadership. Unlike many authors who produce books about leadership, Pepe has never been the director of a public company. Instead, his insight comes from the work he has done as a business facilitator. For over twenty years Pepe has helped mid and large-sized companies and organizations of all sizes to develop their operations and improve their leadership through facilitation. Pepe is a true facilitation pioneer, and he leads by example. He embraces mistakes as learning opportunities and isn't afraid to share the lessons he learns from them.

Pepe's advice has been very crucial in my success as a facilitative leader. When I became the Managing Director at Grape People, Pepe emphasised that shared workshops are important, but one-on-one meetings are equally important as leadership opportunities. That is where you truly ensure that things are heading in the right direction.

This book is based around different types of meetings and workshops which Pepe calls *Key moments of a facilitative leader*. These are the same as what we put into practice to successfully lead. At Grape People we use a set annual development cycle in which certain facilitatory leadership situations recur predictably. For example, our entire staff participates in the annual strategy update in August. It is a truly participatory event which draws on everyone's skills and perspectives to create a shared direction and strategic solutions for the coming years. The owners and board members are present, so the official approval of the strategy later on is simply a formality. The rest of the year continues in a similar way, with each month or so bringing with it different strategy sessions, progress meetings, and workshops. After the strategy update meetings, I hold personal meetings with everyone to review their goals for the next six months. In this book, Pepe details the coaching model which is excellent for situations like these. Afterwards, we all meet up again in September to think about how we can support one another in achieving our goals. The first strategy follow-up session is in October, when we review how the strategy we set in August is working, expand on solutions, and solidify and update our procedures. As part of the procedures, we have agreed on our own development workshops several months in advance to work on the strategy's areas for improvement. This book will teach you a model for facilitating workshops like these. This predictable structure of workshops and meetings is called an *annual leadership cycle*. This book will help you to consider your own organisation's annual leadership cycle, and I am thrilled that all of Pepe's methods that he has refined over the years to facilitate key leadership moments are now available to all.

This is an extremely practical handbook for all team leaders, supervisors, managers and directors who wish to highlight the competence of their employees and partners, continually improve productivity, and create commitment to common goals. Is it possible to act as a supervisor and lead a team without using the advice in this book? Perhaps, but that would be a longer journey full of trial and error. Pepe has already taken this journey for you in his decades of experience, and he packages the most effective tools into a convenient and easy-to-learn format. You will be able to start effectively using facilitatory leadership techniques immediately.

PIRITTA VAN DER BEEK
June 14th, 2018
Helsinki, Finland

ABOUT THE AUTHOR

Pepe Nummi has led international and virtual teams since 1990 and worked as a facilitator since 1998. He has served as the inaugural chairman of the Finnish Association of Facilitators. Pepe is a facilitation trailblazer and is one of the founders of the company Grape People; a company that focuses on facilitation training and services for businesses around the world. On top of all this, Pepe is the developer of the idealogue method, and is the author of *The Handbook on Facilitation* (2007), *The Handbook of Virtual Facilitation* (2012), and *Beyond Brainstorming – Idealogue* (2016). Over the course of his long career he has provided facilitation services in over 20 countries and has also trained over 10,000 facilitators.

ACKNOWLEDGEMENTS

I did not write this book alone, that would have been impossible. The content was developed together with my colleagues Piritta van der Beek, Miikka Penttinen, Kari Kukkola and Jonas Lindström. I received practical advice from great Organisational Development professionals Amanda Stott, Nina Laaksonen, Yue Jiao Dong, and Jean-Philippe Poupard. Andrew Ullom gave me his professional support in writing and editing the book. Finally, all of the methods and ways of working that are presented in this book have been tested and refined in co-operation with the participants of my workshops.

INTRODUCTION

We begin our journey by joining a discussion between the Fruit &
Loading Inc. Sales Team Leader Susanna Swan and her old friend
George Moose, who is a professional facilitator.

George and Susanna were enjoying their morning tea together when a
question popped into George's mind. He looked at Susanna and asked,
"If there was a fight between a lion and a tiger, which one would win?"

George's eccentric nature was nothing new to Susanna, so the
seemingly random question did not catch her completely off guard.
She pondered her answer while chewing on a pink macaroon.
"Well, I guess they are about the same size...but they do call the
lion the *king of the jungle*, so I think that the lion beats the tiger."
George laughed. He knew more about this than his original question
indicated. "In ancient Rome during the gladiatorial competitions, the
Romans often matched a lion versus a tiger and had them fight for
sport. The Romans bet large sums of money on these competitions of
course, it was part of the fun for them. And guess what, most of the
money was placed on the tiger to win."

This legitimately shocked Susanna, and, with eyebrows raised, she
asked, "Really?"

"It's true," George assured her. "The tiger was favoured to win. This is because when pitted against each other, the tiger took advantage of the lion's nature. Tigers are ruthless and go straight for the kill. Compare this to the lion, which is more inquisitive and reserved, almost friendly when compared to the tiger."

Susanna considered this bit of information while George continued on.

"Now think of five lions versus five tigers. Which group wins this battle?"

"The lions," Susanna answered confidently. "I know that lions are group animals and they work well together, while tigers are more of the loner type."

"You're absolutely right, Susanna! It reminds me of the famous story from the Rotterdam zoo. In 1934, the zoo purchased a group of big cats that was made up of, you guessed it, lions and tigers. While the zoo was preparing the separate habitats for the animals, they were kept in temporary accommodations quite close to each other. Unfortunately, being around so many other big cats made all the lions and tigers quite anxious which of course led to a fight."

Listening to this, Susanna couldn't help but wonder how their nice breakfast conversation had turned to cat fights throughout history, and her mind began to drift.

"Stay with me Susanna! I'm going somewhere with this, I promise. Anyways, one lion and one tiger began fighting, but the difference between the two animals was this; once the fight began, all the tigers looked uninterested, while *every single lion* leapt in and attacked the tiger, killing it."

Susanna gasped. This conversation was beginning to become a bit graphic for tea time.

George continued, growing more and more enthusiastic. "And the lions did not stop there! They managed to get into the tiger enclosure and attack the rest of the tigers, on by one, until the job was finished and only lions remained. The lions were acting as a synchronized unit focused on a common goal, strong and unified, while the tigers perished individually."

Tea time continued as Susanna steered the conversation back to easier topics. It was only weeks later that she realized George was not talking about lions or tigers, he was talking about work.

At work many different types of animals can be identified; we have the bull who charges recklessly ahead towards his goals, smashing anything that gets in the way. On the other hand, we have the rabbit; quick, nimble, quiet, and barely noticeable. In your office you probably even have a sloth or two.

And then there are the animals at the top of it all, the leaders. Those that are in control of the environment. A manager or leader who can be called a tiger may accomplish objectives. They have their idea of a goal or strategy and everyone else in the environment needs to bend and conform to that. This gets results, but in an archaic, top-down fashion. Then there are the lions. Every group of lions has a leader, but the group is unified, working towards a common goal and identifying the needs of others and responding to those needs effortlessly. This book is about forming and maintaining groups that work productively towards a common purpose.

There are thousands of titles claiming to provide the key to leading well. And a lot of the information in these books is valid and effective. But still, most of these books have a fatal flaw; they provide tips and tools to lead individuals instead of groups, which creates tigers.

There is an alternative way to lead; facilitative leadership. Facilitative leadership is a participatory way of guiding a group. It focuses on developing self-recognition of the whole system on the individual level. When this is achieved there are no questions about the motives of the group, or if there are alignment issues between group members. It is about getting everyone in the same room, creating mutual understanding of goals and co-operation, and reviewing work processes in order to have a common, shared way of working.

A culture of co-operation is created most effectively when people get together and communicate directly, not when they work in isolation. This book does not make the mistake of focusing on self-leadership or leading individuals one-by-one. Instead, this book gives a complete and balanced picture of leadership by explaining and demonstrating how to lead groups of people.

The Handbook of Facilitative Leadership: Concrete Ways to Boost Performance does not claim that all leadership situations require facilitation techniques. Instead, it covers nine key leadership moments and demonstrates the specific application of leadership tools and techniques as each situation requires. What kind of activities lead to the best understanding of common goals? How should meetings be structured to create the best intergroup dynamic? How are different themes, goals, and tasks integrated by systematic leadership? These questions will be answered by the different leadership situations and analysis that are presented in each chapter. The examples come by telling the story of our friend Susanna Swan, a manager and team leader who works for the logistics firm Fruit & Loading Inc., located on the 23rd floor of a skyscraper overlooking the heart of London. Susanna's story centres on the leadership situations she has with her team where they deploy company strategy, brainstorm, resolve interpersonal conflicts, and more. These situations give Susanna the opportunity to examine and resolve some of the most common challenges faced by team leaders. Each chapter of the book presents a common leadership situation and practical solutions for how to handle it. The final chapters summarise the key skills needed in virtual environments and explain how to use the tools systematically.

This book explains how to lead both in virtual and face-to-face situations. Successful leadership happens when people connect, which make meetings key leadership opportunities. Poor meeting practices that hinder traditional face-to-face business interactions have made their way into a technologically challenging virtual world, where they have become even worse. Meeting leaders have less control in virtual environments which can result in participants becoming more likely to lose focus and begin multitasking, instead of paying attention and contributing. And can you blame them? A lot of virtual meetings amount to participants waiting idly as they listen to a muddled voice come through their laptop speaker. Instead of engaging, they end up waiting for their turn to talk. Leadership techniques and communication tools that work in traditional face-to-face meetings do not always translate well to virtual environments, which can lead to directionless, ineffective leadership. *The Handbook of Facilitative Leadership: Concrete Ways to Boost Performance* presents challenges faced when leading virtually and also in the traditional face-to-face working environment.

The nine key moments of a facilitative leader presented in this book are:

- Kickoff meeting
- Implementing goals
- Supporting goal implementation with coaching
- Problem solving workshop
- Stakeholder communication plan
- Team development: increasing collaboration
- Team development: agreeing on ground rules
- Team development: celebrating success
- Progress meeting

And finally, the *Handbook of Facilitative Leadership: Concrete Ways to Boost Performance* is all about boosting team performance. Without the proper implementation of the right leadership tools the team will not reach its full potential.

CHAPTER 1:

INTRODUCING FACILITATIVE LEADERSHIP

Susanna is venting her frustrations to George as they are having lunch in a Coffee shop in central London.

"George, I'm in trouble. I can't find the time to do all the things I need to do at work. And the worst thing is that the more I work, the larger the workload! I send out instructions to my team, thinking that this will give me some time for other job stuff, but for every email I send out, ten questions come back my way. And to top it all off, my boss is becoming more and more demanding He is always pushing me to be more ambitious and produce more than I already am! I'm going crazy. I knew I should have been an apple farmer instead of a business woman."

George laughed at the thought of Susanna as a farmer. He knew that she had a hard-enough time *shopping* for apples. Growing them was out of the question. "Becoming a farmer is a good idea, but I'm sure you would miss London when you are out in the countryside and away from civilization. Anyway, tell me more about the problem. What is actually happening at work?"

"I'm leading a Sales Team that is spread out across a few different countries and time zones. I like my team. The people are not the problem. The problem is how much time it takes to manage them! Today I spent the whole day with key customers, solving their problems. When I opened my computer in the afternoon, I saw forty-five emails, and not even one of them was spam! They all demanded some sort of reply or effort from my end, even if it was just me spending the time to read them. So there went three hours of my life."

Considering this for a moment, George had a suggestion. "Couldn't you go through them and reply later?"

Susanna chuckled at George's naïve question. "I wish, but they were all urgent. This one new salesman from Edinburgh actually sent me fourteen emails in a single day. He has been with us for just one week, and so far, he is a good guy; curious, and eager to learn. He is making great progress with the customers too, but his questions never end. I don't care how good of a salesman he is, he takes too much of my time."

George continued with his questions. "Do you have a big team?"

"Not too big. We have twelve salesmen and three sales secretaries that organize the trips and meetings for the rest of the team."

George was beginning to get an idea of Susanna's situation. "OK, and you oversee everything? It's on you to co-ordinate their work?"

"Yes," Susanna said. "But that is just the beginning."

George did not know what she meant so he asked her to elaborate.

Susanna continued, "I am talking about the other departments that we have to deal with; Production, Marketing, Logistics, Research and Development.... Today the Marketing Department suddenly made a big sale which is great, but that is not their job! Logistics can't seem to deliver goods to one of the key customers, Production complains that we have sold more than they can make, and all of this without even mentioning the biggest headache of all; my boss Bert."

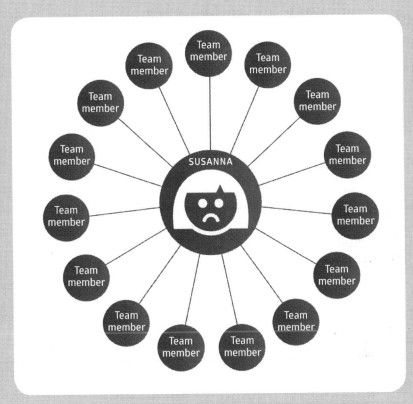

The organizational structure of Susanna and her team. Susanna is the centre of everything, which makes her stressed and unhappy.

George saw that Susanna was starting to turn red and get a bit angry, so he asked her to slow down and just focus on one thing at a time. "Why do you feel that your boss Bert is such a problem?"

Susanna looked at George for a moment and took a deep breath as she prepared herself to list all the problems she has with her boss. "He thinks I should show more leadership with my team because new policy changes and strategies that he pushed for are not going as he would like. He wants the Sales Team to visit customers more often, but the guys just don't have time. I hate my boss. He has no understanding whatsoever about what we are doing. He's completely out of touch with the realities of our job. Imagine a complete stranger walking into your house and beginning to tell you how to organize your furniture. That's what his ideas are like for us. He is so delusional that he even sent me to a leadership training seminar! You know, one of those training programs where they say, 'Be a nice boss!' or 'Give understanding and time to employees.' All that new-age, generalized trash that has no place in the real-world. I have no time to be nicer, I want people to do what I tell them to do and to shut up. Including my boss."

George had known Susanna for quite some time and was used to her getting frustrated now and then. But her most recent outburst surprised him a little. "Wow, I can see that you are struggling. It's difficult to do your job without good leadership and direction from the top down. Are you asked to interact with other people and customers outside of your team? How many key contacts outside of your team do you have?"

"I have to talk with people from outside of the team daily. With the key customers, the other company departments, and some factory representatives..." Susanna paused as she began calculating the total figure. "The outside contacts total around twenty, and if you include the team it is about thirty-five contacts. Nothing too crazy."

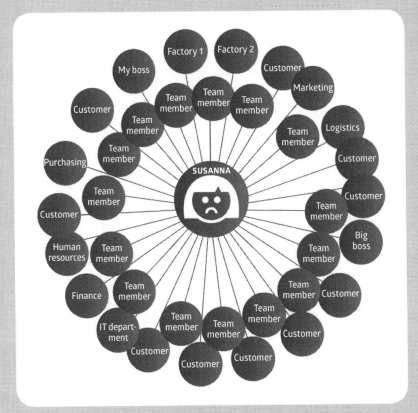

Susanna and her contacts, which include team members, key customers, her boss, and other company employees.

George disagreed. "Thirty-five people. That may not seem like a terribly high amount, but do you know that a group of thirty-five produces over 500 connections within that group?"

Susanna stopped George. "Sorry, I don't follow. What do you mean by *connections*?"

MANAGING TOO MANY CONNECTIONS; WHY LEADERS ARE SO DAMN BUSY

George began to explain. "OK, take you and me talking right now. There is one possible connection, me talking to you. Now, add another person to the mix. Let's call her Mary. I can talk to you, I can also talk to Mary. And finally, you can talk to Mary. This makes three total connections for a group of three people. If you add a fourth person to the group, then there are six total connections. It keeps growing exponentially like that. If we get all the way to thirty-five people, then there are hundreds and hundreds of connections*."

The idea of connections clicked into place for Susanna and she understood how this applied to her work. "I get it, George! Thirty-five is not the number that gives me so much work, but more like 500! That's a lot to manage!"

George agreed. "No wonder you are stressed and feel like you don't have time. You are actually a real miracle worker having to manage so many different connections!"

Susanna smiled, thanked her friend for the compliment, and added, "I should say that it's not always that bad. I'm privileged to be between people which gives me a complete sense of business decisions. I can hear ideas from the top talking to my boss Bert, and I also have constant communication with my Team, so I know how ideas are received as they flow downwards. Sometimes it feels very good to be the only one who has access to all of the information."

"And people appreciate you for that Susanna. They want security. They want to know that someone is in charge."

---

* The exact number of connections in this case is 595. The number of connections grows exponentially for every additional group member added. If there are two people in a group, then there is one connection. If we add a third person to a group of two, then we add two to the amount of connections and get three. Three people equals three connections. Four people equals six connections (three existing connections plus three=six) Five people equals ten connections (six existing connections plus four=ten). Following this math all the way to thirty-five group members, we get 595 connections.

"That is my job as team manager and that's what a leader is, right? Someone who is in charge and in control of a group?"

"It is, but that is just a fraction of the picture. There are many aspects to leading that go beyond being the info-point and a decision maker for a group. When I hear you talk about your problems at work, I see that it is hard for you. It's not a bad thing Susanna. After all, the first step towards solving a problem is acknowledging that the problem exists."

FACILITATIVE LEADERSHIP

Hours have passed already, and George and Susanna are still deep in conversation. George is explaining to Susanna that her team members are overly reliant on using Susanna as an information resource. He proposes a different way of doing things that he thinks will help.

"Susanna, let's step back and talk a moment about what leadership really is. There are hundreds of different leadership theories and thousands of books on the subject, but no definitive agreement about what it is! Thankfully, some broad ideas are generally agreed upon when it comes to leadership. For example, most books and theories agree that leadership is about focusing. Remember the group of lions fighting together against the tigers? This is the type of focus a good leader can give their team. Your key function as a team leader is to give and maintain team direction[*]. When I work with organisations and ask people about their goals, I get a different answer from everyone. People are losing lots of energy without clear direction."

---

[*]   This will be seen when a new strategy is implemented to the Sales Team in the third chapter, called, *Goal Implementation Workshop*. These types of meetings present goals, and then turn the presented material into actionable steps for team members to follow. How to maintain goals will be explained in the tenth chapter called *The Progress Meeting*.

Susanna did not think she was hearing anything important or new. "I know all of that already George, and that is exactly what I'm doing; keeping the team focused on their tasks and goals. It is pretty basic after all, isn't it?"

George was not discouraged by her know-it-all attitude and pushed forward.

"You may be doing this already, but the key is how you influence people to reach their goals. The key difference between leaders, lions and tigers if you will, is in decision making. A tiger does it all from beginning to end. They make the decision, then delegate the tasks to get it done and finally they follow up on everything with each individual. Tigers believe they can focus people by giving orders. A lion is much different. A lion is a facilitative leader that helps everyone on the team make decisions together. Facilitative leadership is helping people see the full picture. And once someone sees the bigger picture, they will have a more complete and true understanding of the situation. And this complete understanding is what brings out an increased focus on the group level."

Susanna paused, as she considered what George had just told her. She understood what George meant, but still had her doubts. After all, isn't an employee supposed to follow instructions and complete the tasks given to them anyway? "George, do my employees really need this 'true understanding' to do their jobs and do what I tell them?"

"Maybe not Susanna, but it goes back to your problem of not having enough hours in the day. Remember the emails you constantly get? A true understanding is the ability to exercise initiative to accomplish daily tasks and to concentrate on the most important aspects of the work. A well-led team does not just follow instructions. Instead, they are familiar enough with the bigger picture to be able to prioritise their work and decide how best to spend their time and energy. High performance is all about creating understanding, direction and alignment. Does all the information and guidance exchanged in the Team need to flow through you? If everyone understood the big picture, people could manage their own connections and be in direct contact with one another and all stakeholders."

Leadership is about focusing people and establishing connections within the group. This allows for information to flow easily and the result is people working towards large goals together.

Susanna thought this over for a moment. "I definitely see how a facilitative style could help. OK, that solves the problem of me being the central connection. But how do I make sure the train is going in the right direction? If everyone decides what they do themselves, who makes sure that there is co-ordinated action? I still need control. After all, I am the boss for a reason, George."

"Of course, and you have to make sure that all team members are pointed in the right direction. That's your key function. But there is another way of accomplishing team alignment besides giving orders," countered George. "You can communicate the goals for team members and let them design and co-ordinate the actions themselves. This is a great way to increase group alignment."

"I see your point George," nodded Susanna.

"And why is group communication important?" asked George, before answering his own question. "Because if people want to be effective, they need to align their work together. Aligning their work means that they need to co-ordinate their tasks and goals and remove obstacles, so they can perform together."

Susanna thought for a moment about what George said and began to express her thoughts. "OK, so if you let the people align their work together, you will probably also find them better motivated and needing less guidance."

THE BENEFITS AND CHALLENGES OF THE TRADITIONAL LEADERSHIP MODEL

Benefits of the traditional leadership model
· Well tested

Challenges with the traditional leadership model
· Employees do not see the big picture
· Does not promote self-leadership and requires guidance and control
· Less participation in decision making → less commitment
· Does not work well with complexity since the leader cannot manage every detail

"Exactly Susanna! It is all about having informed employees that have a solid grasp of company goals and strategic direction. As a team leader you need to create an understanding of the whole system. When you do this, you are creating a team that can shift their priorities when needed, and transition well between projects. An effective leader will make sure that a team can communicate, prioritise and refocus itself without the manager or team leader having to be in the middle of everything. It may sound intimidating and difficult but really, it's not. There are simple tools and steps you can use."

Susanna was becoming intrigued, but she was still a bit worried. "So, what you're saying that I need to always be creating group understanding when acting as a leader at work. The ideas sound nice but the reality of this is that it just creates more for me to do. It's more work and less time, right?"

George did not blame Susanna for being sceptical, and he continued to persuade her. "No, because when you have created common goals and understanding about how the system works, people can coordinate and manage their work themselves. This means less for you to do, and more time to daydream about a cold drink on a warm sunny beach."

The idea of relaxing on white sand beaches got Susanna's attention as she asked George another question. "So, your job as a facilitator is to use facilitative leadership tools and methods?"

THE BENEFITS AND CHALLENGES OF FACILITATIVE LEADERSHIP

Benefits of Facilitative Leadership
- Enables self-leadership
- Helps employees see and understand the big picture
- Increases employee motivation and commitment via participatory decision making
- Helps employees align tasks
- Facilitated meetings can help create innovation and new ideas
- Very effective in dealing with complexity

Challenges of Facilitative Leadership
- Allows idea creation by employees and may seem chaotic
- Requires group facilitation skills to deal with the chaos of group decision making

TAKING THE ROLE OF A FACILITATOR

"Yes, that's right, Susanna. Imagine the chaos if you take fifteen people in a room and ask them all to voice their concerns and ask questions. It simply would not work. Without guidance, groups are not very effective at working together. To help the group work together, the facilitator has a whole range of methods and techniques up their sleeve which they use to successfully lead the group towards finding solutions that everyone is committed to."

"These tools don't take years of practice to learn, do they? Are they easy to get the hang of?"

"Don't worry about the tools Susanna, they are a piece of cake," replied George. "It is taking on the role of a facilitator that is the challenge."

Susanna did not understand what George meant about the role of a facilitator being a challenge and asked him what was so difficult about it.

"The key problem for leaders is to stay neutral. The traditional model for a meeting is a chaired meeting. You know the kind Susanna, where the chairperson runs the meeting entirely. They are the one giving the reports and presenting all the information. But they also decide when to transition from one part of the meeting to the next. This means that the chairperson takes on two roles, being responsible for both the content and the way of working. Yet it's impossible for someone to juggle two roles at once. Time and again the chairperson becomes so involved in the content of the meeting that they no longer notice if the process stops working. A meeting which is firmly led by a chairperson may work efficiently for decision making, but on average a chairperson speaks for around 70 % of the time during a meeting."

Susanna did not see anything wrong with a chairperson dominating a meeting. "But that's the point of the chairperson, right? They need to talk a lot in order to give direction and express new procedures and action plans."

"That can be true, but there is a better way. In meetings where the chairperson speaks for most of the time, people may feel that they are participating in an informative event, which can seem like a waste of time. Like you, a lot of people feel that they are short on time at work, so they start to take care of other tasks instead of actively listening and participating in the meeting. A lot of the time no comments or questions are expected of participants since the important decisions have obviously been made in advance elsewhere."

The value of using facilitation: Chaos is transformed into order and alignment.

"I know that this is not the best way, but its business as usual George. That is just how things go."

As a facilitator, George strongly disagreed with Susanna's 'business as usual' remark. "But Susanna, my whole point is that meetings do not have to be this way! If we all believed in 'business as usual' nothing would evolve, and we still would be cashing paper checks and sending faxes. But innovation and new ways of doing things are what lead to progress and growth. Take facilitation for example. A facilitator is different. They act as a conductor who leads the group in the meeting but remain impartial to content. This impartial role is very difficult for leaders to fill, but very important to guarantee the quality of meetings and workshops."

"A facilitator needs to remain impartial…So you are telling me that I shouldn't tell my Sales Team what to do anymore. This is already sounding impossible," sighed Susanna.

George tried to ease her mind. "It's probably a big change for you, but you shouldn't give directions to your team when you are facilitating the group. Let me give you an example of what not to do. I know this leader of a large engineering company. He has the best experts on earth working for him. But during management meetings he dominates the floor and talks much more than anyone else. Wouldn't it be better if he took a step back and allowed them to have more of a voice? He hired the experts for a reason."

"OK George, you got me there. But I can't just be neutral all the time. Sometimes I need advocate for certain ideas and promote projects. I still have my boss Bert pressuring me to get certain results from the team. But if you can show me some ways I can influence the group as a leader without dominating the meeting and just giving orders, then I am OK with it."

George grins. "Good, now we are getting somewhere Susanna. Believe me when I say that giving up your role as the primary speaker in a meeting who is emotionally invested in the content will not lead to a lack of influence, nor will it hurt your ability to lead. In fact, business leaders worldwide are having to learn how to focus more on the meeting process rather than the content. This is becoming a necessary skill as more and more teams are spread out around the world, and more and more people are choosing to work remotely."

"OK George, I follow. Tell me, a leader who facilitates is the same as a facilitator, right?"

George stops Susanna right there. "Absolutely not. A leader uses facilitative group methods, but only in situations that need it. I call these times *key leadership* situations. For leaders who know facilitation, acting as a facilitator is just a temporary role. They are able to wear many different hats, as you probably know all too well. Compare this to a facilitator, someone usually brought in from outside of the company to help run meetings or resolve conflict. This person is 100 % content neutral and just focuses on the process."

Role of a facilitator

100 % neutral	Helping people bring together and combine ideas

A facilitator is a person who leads group processes and is neutral in regard to content. A group process is a group's way of solving problems, making decisions, resolving conflicts, and communicating. The role of a facilitator is to concentrate solely on the process of the meeting.

"So my only option now is to try being a neutral facilitator in my meetings?"

"I suggest you try the role of a facilitator and you will see your team members come up with good ideas and make fantastic decisions. There are several other options besides taking the role of the facilitator; you can wash your hands completely of the task of facilitation by assigning the role to someone else. Or you may use check-points. There is a potential check-point after each stage. For instance, when the group has clarified the challenges, you may connect the group ideas with your own by adding your own challenges. When the group has created solutions, you connect group solutions with your own. No matter which option you choose, the secret to success is having a content neutral person to manage the meeting process."

"You are a good salesman George. You got me interested in the check-points. What if I facilitate and my team suggests an action plan that I disagree with?"

"You can add or delete action items once they have finished their work. You are the boss after all and if you leave the room without committing to the action plan, nothing is going to happen anyway. Just make sure you appreciate the group work and explain why you can't accept the group suggestions."

- Trust that the group will find the right solutions. Your role is to facilitate and to focus solely on the process.
- Delegate the task of facilitating to another employee.
- Start the meeting by facilitating and only share your own opinions and thoughts on the content after each stage of discussion (if you need to).

There are several different ways to make sure the meeting is well facilitated even when the leader is a content owner.

"That clears it right up, thanks George."

George continues explaining his view of leadership to Susanna. "The core of it is that you help guide people. This is very different from the traditional model where these 'right' conclusions are just handed to employees from the top down. As the leader you don't have to think about the right answers yourself, but rather how you can help people find the right answers. It is a totally different level of thinking and it can sometimes be a difficult adjustment for some leaders and managers to make."

Hearing George call the change from traditional leadership to facilitating the team a 'difficult adjustment' worried Susanna. She frowned and asked, "So you mean to tell me that I might not make it?"

"Don't worry, I will be here to help you every step of the way," laughed George, trying to reassure his friend.

A facilitative leader creates group alignment by using facilitation tools.

VIRTUAL FACILITATION

Now that George has explained a lot more about how facilitative leadership works, Susanna thinks that she can do it, and she knows for a fact that she wants to. But there is one thing that she thinks may ruin everything; most of the time spent with her team is done virtually. Do George's methods work virtually?

"George, you have been talking all about groups and facilitation. Doesn't that require workshops and meetings? My team is spread out across Europe! We have to have meetings where people tele-conference in, so they can hear presentations from management and updates from Team leaders. These types of meetings without people present would be difficult to facilitate, right?"

"Don't be so sure Susanna. I've successfully helped hundreds of teams have dynamic meetings in virtual environments."

At this point Susanna was beginning to get annoyed with her friend. He had a solution for everything! "OK George, I get it. You are a guru who can walk on water and fix any meeting, virtual or not. But I don't know if I can do this."

George laughed. "Well thanks for the compliment, even though I *may* detect some sarcasm I'm not perfect, no one is. And I don't always succeed."

George is not perfect after all, thought Susanna, as she pressured him to tell her the details.

"Once I had a client who wanted to have better virtual meetings. The management team consisting of five or six regional managers and the administration. They all met virtually once a week to see how work was progressing. The CEO talked to everyone one at a time, asking each individual manager about their district, the current challenges, and all of that. While these individual conversations were happening, everyone else was stuck waiting for their turn. Most of the group hated these boring virtual meetings, because they spent about an hour just waiting for the five minutes where they could talk. I explained different methods and ways of working and how the virtual meetings could be activated and made dynamic and interesting, but the CEO was not receptive. We never got to try the methods, as the CEO said he did not want any participatory stuff because the team members always started fighting when they addressed each other or when a question was posed to everyone at once."

Susanna contemplated George's story for a moment and said, "So the CEO wanted to keep control and play the policeman. What an idiot."

"Not exactly. Sometimes control works very well. Especially if you work in a relatively simple environment where the company strategy is easy to keep track of, and where the different teams don't collaborate much. But it is these types of current leadership practices based on control that are impossible in the virtual world. How do you think you can keep someone motivated in other parts of the world if you just control them and you only talk to each other during poorly run meetings? It just does not work. I believe that in virtual environments leadership cannot be based on control, but instead it needs to be based on true understanding and motivation."

"That all sounds nice George, but what about the quality of the meetings? Are you saying that you can really have the same quality of meetings virtually that you do face-to-face?"

Susanna's difficult question forced George to think for a moment. He chose his words carefully, and eventually said, "There are trade-offs, but yes, I do. Technical solutions are never perfect, as they don't provide the same kind of experience that a real face-to-face encounter can. But a virtual meeting can actually work better in some situations than a face-to-face meeting would. Over the course of leading hundreds of virtual meetings, I have realised that people tend to be much more straight-forward and open in virtual meetings[*]. This makes the time of the meetings shorter while increasing output and productivity. Pretty neat, right?"

"That is interesting. I've noticed the same phenomenon in how people use social media," Susanna replied.

George nodded and said, "And most virtual meeting platforms work quite well if you take the time to become familiar with them. Today, good web conference technology is easy to find, and used quite often[**]. The most important feature is to have a whiteboard where everyone can write their ideas and where the group can choose the best ideas. Also, most platforms allow for a main conference room to be split into smaller rooms for discussion and work in pairs or small groups, which is fantastic."

---

[*] People are more direct in virtual meetings because they are able to separate themselves more from the content of the meetings and see things more objectively. This trend is put to use by facilitators by using group memory, which is talked about in chapter 8.

[**] There are many different options a business has when choosing which platform to use for hosting virtual meetings, and the options continue to grow daily. This handbook doesn't concentrate on any specific technological platform or program. Instead we'll tell you how to lead effective virtual meetings without mentioning any specific platform or program by name. The methods presented are suitable for all platforms with voice and whiteboard functions, which can be found on most meeting hosting platforms such as Skype for business, WebEx Training Center and Adobe Connect Pro. These programs also include functions such as chats or polling (voting), which play a role in some of the exercises and techniques presented in this book.

THE MOST IMPORTANT FEATURES OF A VIRTUAL MEETING PLATFORM

1. Whiteboard (or any place where all participants can write simultaneously)
   · for visualising and prioritising ideas
2. Break-out rooms
   · for small group-work

Susanna was sold and wanted to get past the generalities and learn how to use the principles of facilitation. "OK, I get it. It is possible to facilitate and lead effectively both virtually and face-to-face. Now just tell me how to actually do it."

SUMMARY

This chapter introduced the concept of facilitative leadership; a participatory practice of guiding the group and helping the group make decisions. When the team members are in the same place at the same time and make decisions together, they create an understanding of the larger picture and become capable of aligning activities and leading themselves. Communication in large groups can be challenging, which makes facilitative leadership a key to success.

By applying facilitative leadership methods, you will find it easier to focus the team on goals, solve performance barriers, align actions, and increase team cohesiveness which leads to better performance. This is possible even in virtual meetings when using the right platform and ways of working.

Now let's find out how to do it in practice.

A FACILITATIVE LEADER...

- · aids group decision making in order to support mutual learning, to make sure of commitment, and to ensure concrete decisions and actions.
- · takes part in decision making and does not allow the group to make decisions when he/she is not committed.
- · focuses on matters that are essential for the success of the group (which are presented in the chapters of this book) and which require both commitment and mutual learning. Everything does not need to be facilitated.
- · is content neutral in order to ensure group effectiveness and participation. This role may be delegated to other group members.

Facilitative leadership in a nutshell.

CHAPTER 2:

THE KICKOFF MEETING

Six months have passed since her long conversation with George about leadership and facilitation, and a lot has changed since they spoke. Fruit & Loading Inc. has been thriving as of late. Susanna, acting as Sales Manager, has attended several leadership and facilitation courses and she has been off to a good start. So far, she has had the chance to facilitate brainstorming events and strategic and general meetings that have taken place in the London office.

The business landscape has changed too, unfortunately for the worse. The economy is in crisis, and uncertain conditions overshadow Fruit & Loading Inc. Nobody really knows what the future holds. The situation has created doubt and instability within the company, and Fruit & Loading Inc. has responded by shifting focus from the development of product and projects to concentrating on immediate problems and holding emergency meetings. The financial strain has even forced Susanna's boss and Fruit & Loading Inc.'s director Bertram Upper-Thrapplewaite to place company-wide bans on new training initiatives and travel. Known by friends and close colleagues as Bert, he is a passionate man who loves both fruits and smart business decisions. Considering his passions, Fruit & Loading Inc. is extremely important to him and he always wants to know what is going on around the company. Bert also needs to always have his say when it comes to decision making. He is very demanding of his employees, but he is fair and willing to listen to the voice of reason when he is wrong.

One rainy Monday morning Susanna is sipping her green apple tea at her desk. Despite a sizeable workload, she wears a blank stare on her face as she gazes at her computer screen procrastinating. Suddenly, her phone rings. It hasn't rung for at least an hour even though everyone appears to be running themselves ragged with more work to do than ever before.

The greeting "Hi, Susanna" comes from the other end of the phone. Susanna curses her bad luck as she tries to act as cheerful as possible. The voice on the phone belongs to none other than her passionate, but sometimes difficult-to-work-with boss, Bert.

"There's that travel ban in place, but the salesmen need to hold a strategy meeting about the economic crisis. I heard some guys from Powerline Ltd. talking in the lift about attending a virtual meeting."

Virtual meeting...what a mouthful, thought Susanna as Bert continued on.

"Everyone in the company is nervous because they have heard rumours about a new company strategy and they suspect budget cuts and increased sales targets. Robson from Finance and I have done some new calculations and now it looks as though we're going to have to let at least two offices go; St. Petersburg, and Seville. You're going to facilitate an event with your Sales Team where we can constructively discuss the final decision together. But remember, we don't have the funds to invite the whole Sales Team to London. Instead, we're going to have to hold an online meeting. It's your job to facilitate the event."

In a normal situation, the whole team would fly to Fruit & Loading Inc.'s central office in London where Susanna would lead a workshop to discuss the issue at hand. The whole Sales Team would have the chance to reflect on matters and consider their feelings about the new changes and any possible solutions.

Well there go the coffee breaks and nice chit-chat, thought Susanna as she considered Bert's demands. What worried Susanna even more than the potential loss of her cherished coffee breaks was having to run a workshop without being able to use her familiar dry-erase pen and whiteboard. She was used to drawing, taking notes, and constantly writing information and key points down for all to see during the meetings and workshops she led. She knew how to lead meetings in face-to-face situations. *Didn't Bert see how well the kickoff meeting went with upper management?!* thought Susanna, as she processed Bert's request. Susanna had zero experience leading virtual meetings and making matters worse was Susanna's personal history of disappointment and struggles with technology. Using new programs or devices always seemed to be harder than it should be for Susanna, and things often did not work like they should. She frantically searches for reasons to refuse.

"But Bert, people have got to be together in person if you want to achieve real dialogue. You've seen so yourself when I've facilitated face-to-face meetings."

"If you want to keep your job, you had better figure out how we can get our salesmen to communicate without leaving their offices," Bert threatens.

Suddenly, the words of George come to Susanna's mind and she remembers his advice. "The basic ideas and methods of facilitation can be adapted to a virtual environment. You just have to get a platform that works online and remember to focus intently on the process of the meeting."

Armed with these words she gathers the courage to reluctantly accept the job. She promises Bert that she will try to find out more about how virtual facilitation works. She turns on her computer and starts browsing to see if there is something about virtual facilitation. To her surprise, Susanna finds several virtual meeting platforms and lots of technical training to help users. Sadly, there isn't much information or training on holding virtual meetings.

I suppose I'll just have to develop my own methods, Susanna thinks to herself.

Susanna carries on her research by looking through facilitation books for the rest of the week, all the while thinking of the kind of technical platform which would be the best choice for Fruit & Loading Inc. Susanna finds that most methods and tools she has used in her face-to-face workshops in the past can be adapted for use in virtual meetings. This motivates her, and she pushes onwards.

If I want to look like I know what I'm doing at all, I'll just have to create an even more accurate plan and stick to it; at least at first. The technology will probably pose its own challenges too, she thinks.

As her research continues, Susanna's mood gradually changes, and she even begins to feel a small bit of enthusiasm. Her mind fills with thoughts of virtual group work and energising tools. Soon she sees visions of the meetings of the future; participants scattered around the world, chatting in real-time, discussing ideas all while sharing screen shots and sending images to better explain their thoughts. The technology is intuitive and easy to use, and everyone is happy. She can see drawings of the faces of colleagues she hasn't seen in years. She dreams of applying suntan lotion to her arms all while holding a virtual meeting on a sun-kissed beach in Bali, far away from the cold wind and slush of winter.

Optimism has fully replaced pessimism and Susanna is pleased. Perhaps something good will come out of this economic crisis. Perhaps it will provide a basis for totally new kinds of meetings. After a restless night, Susanna returns to the office and flicks through the instruction manual that came with the virtual meeting platform that she recently purchased. *It's not as difficult as I imagined*, she concludes. Susanna is on her way to leading her first virtual meeting.

CHECKING THE TECHNOLOGY

Welcome to our discussion event Susanna taps out in the title field of an e-mail. She continues to write;

The company has had to make some far-reaching strategic decisions. You are invited to discuss them in an online workshop at 9:00am on October 3rd. Everyone participating should test out their technology with me in advance on the day before the meeting at 3:00pm. You can check your technology by clicking the following link at 3:00pm on October 2nd. The link will log you into our virtual meeting room, and once you have logged in, you can make sure everything works, and say hello to the rest of the team.

On October the 2nd, everybody checked their technology per Susanna's wishes except for Rita Barmyfield. Rita had already promised Susanna that she would participate from Slovenia, where she's spending her autumn holiday, but there appears to be a problem as she is nowhere to be found. Everyone else is online, exchanging greetings with each other.

Kevin Fitzgerald remarked, "Well look at this, I haven't talked to all of you at once since I was in London two years ago for our annual party!"

"This is a pleasant surprise. Everything is working fine, and I can hear all of you-even though I am on the train on my way home," adds Matthew Stevens.

Susanna finishes the testing session by showing her gratitude to everyone who managed to successfully log on to check the technology. "Thank you all for testing out your equipment. Now we don't need to waste time configuring things tomorrow. See you then."

Even Rita manages to fix her connectivity problems by going to a nearby internet café, where she was able to find a computer and log into the meeting room.

According to Susanna's friend George, testing the technology beforehand is one of the best practices when working in the virtual world. There are always technical problems, especially if it's your first virtual meeting, and the meeting can be delayed if problems occur because you haven't tested your technology in advance.

To end the day Susanna compiles a PowerPoint presentation on her process which she will show to the participants during the workshop. First, she chooses a method to start with. A real meeting is like a taking a flight; you must check in before you take off.

CHECK-IN

TASK 1:
Welcome to the virtual meeting

Please draw a picture of yourself (click the pen tool on the toolbar at the bottom of the page)

Susanna's opening slide for the virtual meeting that welcomes participants and gives instructions for the check-in process. Many virtual platforms allow people to write and draw on slides.

The next morning Susanna is at the office bright and early, waiting for everyone to get logged in and online. When almost everyone is settled in, Susanna flicks to the welcome slide of her presentation. It asks each participant to draw a picture of themselves in the empty box on their screen. Problems immediately arise.

"My computer won't let me choose a pen," says Sarah Paige.

Rita Barmyfield can't get her phone to work again. As Susanna tries to solve Rita's problem, she helps the others select the pen tool and colours. Soon enough, the issues disappear as quickly as they came, and portraits begin to appear on the screen. A busy silence fills the virtual meeting room as the Fruit & Loading Inc. Sales Team draw themselves using online tools.

After a few minutes Susanna points the cursor at the portraits and asks the participants to reveal their names and where they're calling from.

Before anyone can reply, the sound of apples being packed into boxes can be heard clearly on Kevin Fitzgerald's line. Susanna asks Kevin to close the office door or find a quieter place. Finally, Rita joins the line too; this time her phone was accidentally on silent. With everyone online and engaged, the meeting can begin. And on time, too, much to Susanna's delight.

Before Bert's presentation, Susanna decided that she needed to give the group a few ground rules to follow. First, she mentions patience.

"Sometimes small things go wrong during virtual meetings. Your battery can run out, the connection can fail, or a program just won't work. These things are unavoidable, but if you're patient enough you'll manage, and the problem will be fixed soon."

Then Susanna explains how to use the mute button, which is useful if background noise is preventing you from participating in the workshop. Susanna also emphasises that participation in this workshop is just as important as participating in a live event. As such, it's a good idea to tell your colleagues that you are in a meeting, even though you're attending from your desk. Susanna ends by saying that it's always good to first state your own name when addressing the group so that the rest of the group knows who is talking. Susanna finds that rule to be the hardest, and she's always forgetting it herself.

Virtual Meeting Ground Rules

Mute the line when necessary

Be here (100 %)

Virtual patience

State your name
before you present your ideas to the group

Susanna's ground rules for the virtual meeting.

Susanna goes through the agenda for the day and asks participants to write down their expectations regarding the content.

"Rose Middleton here. I've lost my text twice," she says from the other end of the line.

"Me too. When I've written some text down, it disappears," says another, stating his name as an afterthought. "Waldemar Wurthenberger."

Susanna keeps calm and does her best to introduce the participants to the new tools. Luckily, she held a test meeting last weekend with George.

The participants' expectations begin to appear on the screen:

Hopefully they'll finally tell us whether the company has bit the bullet or not.

Tell us who's going to be fired and who gets to stay.

It's total chaos. Leadership needs to solve the problems.

I want to constructively discuss how to move forward.

I want the chance to give candid feedback and get everything off my chest.

Susanna isn't surprised by the negative atmosphere. Luckily there was some interest and a faint glimmer of hope among the doom and gloom.

Rita, participating from Slovenia, adds, "The main thing is to discuss our feelings and talk about how to move on from this bad spot we are in now."

Susanna thanks the participants for a successful check-in and explains that they are all in the right place to begin addressing their concerns and worries. It's time to start the presentation.

PRESENTATION AND REFLECTION

Before Bert begins his presentation, Susanna instructs everyone on how they can effectively listen.

"After the meeting we'll think about key facts, our feelings on the presentation, its practical significance and concrete procedures. You may write down your thoughts using the chat during the presentation," she suggests.

Bert starts his PowerPoint presentation and begins to explain the changes.

"As a result of the financial situation and bad apple harvests we have no choice but to change our strategy. Our budget will be reduced by 50% and the number of customer visits will be increased by 25% for our entire Sales Team. Unfortunately, we're also going to have to close our St. Petersburg and Seville offices. The Sales Staff that worked from these offices will be able to continue in their same roles by working remotely from home."

The lines are silent. One line begins to crackle.

"You're breaking up, I missed half of what you said," shouts Tony Dingle.

It turns out that Tony had gone to the loading dock with his phone to take care of an urgent apple-related matter. Luckily Bert had written the important text down on a PowerPoint slide, and Susanna asks Tony to read it once he returns to his computer. She asks the participants to tell the entire group if they need to leave the workshop in the future. She reminds everyone that it's best to prepare for the meeting so that you aren't distracted by work, or the temptation of a mid-meeting coffee break.

Bert continues on by presenting the pages and pages of background information he has concerning the strategy and the new organisational changes.

To make sure that the group is still focused on the presentation, Susanna interrupts for a moment and asks everyone to write a short comment on Bert's presentation using the chat. After this, an active discussion on the presentation spontaneously begins on the chat.

Bert finishes his presentation and it is high time for a short break, so people can refill their coffee mugs. After fifteen minutes, the participants return refreshed and ready for discussion.

DISCUSSION

Susanna asks the participants to press the green tick on their computer to indicate that they are back and ready to continue with the meeting. This task is a way for her to check that everyone has returned from the break and are ready to continue. Since everyone seems to be present, Susanna asks the group to write the most important facts from the presentation on the virtual whiteboard.

"Take three minutes to think about what the presentation was about. When you have some ideas, write down the key points of the presentation on the virtual whiteboard."

Susanna remembers to say how much time is given to complete the task. The time limit helps everyone realize the scope of what the facilitator wants them to write, be it an essay, or just a few brief comments. The whiteboard fills up, and a surprised Bert says happily, "It feels like they actually listened."

There is indeed a lot of information about Bert's presentation, not just about the reorganisation, but also about the company's new strategic policy. Once the group filled up the whiteboard with key information from the meeting, Susanna brings up a slide. It contains a chart with axes labelled with plus and minus signs.

Attitude test

My attitude towards change; choose a place on the chart with your cursor

A slide used to elicit participant reaction to an idea or proposal.

"How does everyone feel about the presentation and the changes that were announced? Please point your cursors to the place on the chart which best describes your feelings. On the upper-left of the page you can see a large plus, with the words 'highly positive'. Place your cursor here if your feelings match. On the lower-right, we have the other end of the spectrum which is 'highly negative'. If you feel very down about the presentation, you would place your cursor here. And in between is the middle ground where your cursor goes if you fill a mixture of the two."

Cursors begin to appear on the screen. Two participants, Billy Campbell and Minna Adams, are having trouble. Their cursors aren't on the screen. The sound of furious typing can be heard in the background. Susanna asks where in the world Billy and Minna have gotten to.

"Sorry Susanna, we just got so caught up in things and had so much to say that I sent Minna a private message in the chat."

So that's where the real discussions are taking place! Susanna realised.

Susanna asks if they would like to share their feelings with the others.

Minna says, "These changes have been imminent for a year now and everyone has been scared of getting fired. It's great that a decision has finally been made."

A long discussion on everyone's feelings and emotions follows, and each person has the chance to speak about the pros and cons that the changes will bring.

Susanna is satisfied and smiles as she thinks to herself, *Finally, the Team was able to get things off their chests, and in a virtual environment!* Susanna originally thought that virtual meetings would be less effective and more time consuming than face-to-face meetings. Susanna has learned from her virtual facilitation guide that participants take around one hour to learn how to use a new tool. Once the participants have learned how to use the virtual meeting platform, they are able to participate more freely, confidently, and creatively.

Susanna feels that the group is ready to move on to the third question; the significance of the changes Bert announced. Her tool of choice for this is group work. Susana displays a slide with clear instructions about how the group work will be conducted. Slides like these clearly address any questions or uncertainty that people may have when beginning a new activity.

Reflection in groups:
The practical significance of changes

- The aim of the task is to crystalize the practical significance of changes
- Three whiteboards open
- The groups are ....
- The conference number for the first group is 586-93857667
- The number for the second group is 586-93336611
- The third group will stay on this line
- Groups will write down their discussion on the white board and then summarise the discussion
- In 30 minutes we will present the summaries to the entire group
- If you have problems, write in the chat or call 057-99966668 (Susanna)

Susanna's slide which gives instructions for group work.

Further helping Susanna's cause of introducing a new tool is the virtual meeting technology itself. It's extremely easy to organise group work when using virtual meeting platforms. At the press of a button, the group can be divided into sub-groups for exercises and small group discussion.

"Next I'd like you to think about how the new strategy will affect your own work and the entire workplace."

In her experience as a facilitator, Susanna knows that this is the phase that is the most important for getting results. After all, understanding and accepting how a change affects you personally will create a behaviour change. First, she gives the participants a few minutes to make notes by themselves. Then she divides them up into three groups in which they can think about their solutions together. She gives them half an hour for group discussion and asks each group to choose one member of their group to take notes on the virtual whiteboard.

While the groups spend the given time discussing and brainstorming, Susanna visits each of the groups' chat rooms. She watches for a moment trying not to disturb them with her presence.

"Good thing you came. Our whiteboard keeps disappearing every now and again," snaps Rose, who is a little frustrated because it's her responsibility to write on the board.

Susanna helps the group with their technical problem and they move on.

She realises the importance of guiding a group in the virtual world as well as in the real one. Even though the groups brainstorm and discuss independently, the passive presence of the meeting leader gives a feeling of support and security. The meeting leader also can re-ignite a fading discussion.

Finally, the small groups return to the main group discussion. They examine all of the whiteboards and suggestions, paying attention to the similarities between the suggested actions and the ideas that the small groups had shared with everyone. The whole group had thought up plenty of ideas about the new company strategy and improving communication between employees.

Susanna's thoughts wandered to what will happen after the meeting, and she is already feeling a bit proud of the results. The Sales Team seems to have accepted the difficult issue of the office closures, and the group seems to have come to a common understanding which will help Fruit & Loading Inc. move forward.

In the fourth and final phase, the participants put things into practice. Susanna asks everyone to take three minutes to think about what the next steps are to begin implementing the new strategy. What concrete actions they will carry out and when?

Finally, Susanna asks each participant to write action points in the chat. Bert seems to be very enthusiastic about this, and he puts down eight of his own actions in the chat.

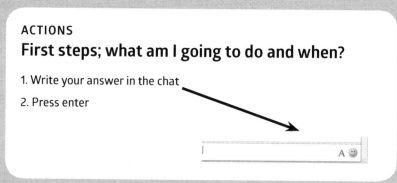

ACTIONS
First steps; what am I going to do and when?

1. Write your answer in the chat
2. Press enter

A slide where group members can share their action points in the group chat.

CHECK-OUT

Susanna believes that it's good etiquette for each person to have a chance to speak when they arrive to a meeting and again when they leave, so she makes sure to include a closing activity which requires participation from everyone.

"I think we all can agree that today's workshop has been very eventful. You have overcome irritation and confusion, and even managed to list concrete actions that can be taken in response to the big changes. I want to say good job to every one of you. How do you feel now?"

At this stage, the reflection stage, Susanna uses the hand icon in her virtual application. The person who wishes to speak raises their virtual hand or clicks the icon in their toolbar*. Tony is first to raise his virtual hand.

"This has been a good experience. I even took care of a couple of work matters too, even though that wasn't the idea. Things are really crazy here in the Seville office. Even though I had to do some work during the meeting I feel way less stress now about the office closing than I did before today's session."

---

* A participant can indicate their willingness to talk by writing their name in the chat when they are ready, or by using similar 'hand raising' features included in many virtual meeting platforms.

From the idyllic mountain villages of Slovenia Rita adds, "I have to admit I felt nervous learning how to use the new tool in advance, especially when there's this crisis at work and I'm far away on holiday. Luckily the telephone connection worked in the end and I was able to attend remotely."

Alfonso Lopez joins in. "It's a good thing that we all know each other here. Otherwise getting to know everyone would have taken a long time and I don't think I would have been so comfortable sharing my feelings with just anyone."

Good comments, Susanna thinks to herself. Originally Susanna had broken into a cold sweat at the mere thought of using virtual tools, but now she feels that the virtual meeting produced results comparable to those of a live meeting.

The virtual meeting saved time, money, and even the environment. The carbon footprint of Fruit & Loading Inc. was drastically smaller for the day, considering what it would cost to bring the entire gang from around the world down to HQ in downtown London. *Just a few more virtual meetings and maybe the company can start holding recreation days again!* Susanna smiles and makes a mental note to do the calculations later to see how much savings virtual meetings can produce, so that she has some ammunition to use when she speaks to Bert about the possibility of a holiday bonus.

ANALYSIS: KICKOFF MEETINGS IN VIRTUAL AND FACE-TO-FACE SETTINGS

After the virtual kickoff meeting, Susanna retreats to her lakeside cabin to reflect on how the day went. She did not know what to expect before facilitating her first virtual meeting, but she quickly learned that it was not too different from how she would conduct a face-to-face meeting. The core structure of both face-to-face and virtual meetings is the same. First, she warms the group up by giving them a small task to break the ice and get everyone comfortable. Then she gives time for the presentation and group reflection. Finally, she ends both the virtual and face-to-face kickoff meetings with a check-out phase.

The structure of Susanna's virtual kickoff meeting

Pre-Meeting
- Check the technology: A virtual check-in before the meeting to familiarize everyone with the technology.

Check-in
- Self Portrait activity
- Ground rules
- Participants comment on their expectations for the day

Presentation and reflection
- Presentation
- Group discussion based on the four parts of the cycle of perception. Each part is discussed one at a time and in sequence: Key facts, Feelings, Meaning and Actions

Check-out
- Comments and feedback from meeting participants by virtual hand raising

The aim of a kickoff meeting is to help participants understand what is presented, discuss it, and produce actionable steps that will be followed up on, and the three-part structure helped Susanna build and lead an effective meeting.

CHECK-IN

The first stage of the meeting is called the check-in phase which is used to get everyone comfortable and ready to actively listen and participate for the entire meeting.

Think of the check-in phase like arriving to the airport, receiving your boarding pass, and dropping off your bags. These things all prepare the traveler for the journey ahead. The idea of the check-in phase for virtual meetings is similar. It prepares participants to enter the virtual world. It is important for everyone to say something out loud so that other participants recognise each other over the phone and become used to speaking in a new situation. Virtual meetings may be a brand-new experience for some people and the check-in phase effectively breaks the ice and prepares people to participate.

Active participation during the first phase calms down any nervous participants and makes it easier to speak out loud for the duration of the meeting. Check-in tools also diminish any dead time that may occur at the start of the meeting due to people signing in late or troubleshooting technical issues. Susanna decided to begin the check-in phase by asking people to draw self-portraits of themselves. She thought that this activity would allow people to get used to the meeting software and relax. It was also an individual task that people could work on while waiting for others to log into the virtual software.

The check-in process also includes listing participants' expectations and reviewing the agenda for the day. It's also good to check that everyone is 100 % present and ready before the meeting, especially just before the presentation phase.

Susanna noticed that the starting phase is very difficult in the virtual world. This is the phase where the facilitator has to create trust which will continue to affect the group atmosphere throughout the entire process. During this initial phase, Susanna's goals are to guide people along the process of the meeting and create trust. Creating trust makes for a safe environment where people have the courage to speak their mind and share ideas.

CHECK-IN

- A meeting practice which helps meeting participants warm up their voices and break the ice as the meeting starts.
- The facilitator can immediately introduce an interactive working method to the group. If you intend to hold a meeting with good participation, the group has to speak within the first five minutes.
- The aim of the Check-in tool is to prepare everyone to enter the virtual world.
- Check-in can also act as a nice activity to keep people occupied as they wait for everyone to arrive and be ready to begin the meeting.
- Good starting practices also include getting to know each other, listing expectations, and explaining the agenda for the day.

The key components of the check-in phase.

Susanna's pre-meeting preparation for the virtual meeting was more extensive, and probably even more important than how she prepares for face-to-face meetings. Susanna needed to test out the technology beforehand and have everyone check-in virtually to demonstrate that they would be able to attend virtually when the day came. This pre-meeting preparation is vital for both the facilitator and the meeting attendees. It is also a good idea for the facilitator to test out all of the slides and moving parts of the technological platform to familiarize themselves and ensure that everything is working as it should.

PRESENTATION

The presentation phase is the informational phase of the process; the distribution of information or content to the participants. Core issues are presented during the presentation, and afterwards they are discussed and expanded on by the group. In order to keep participants focused, it's a good idea to add short refreshing tasks like discussing things in the chat virtually or in small groups or asking for feedback throughout the presentation.

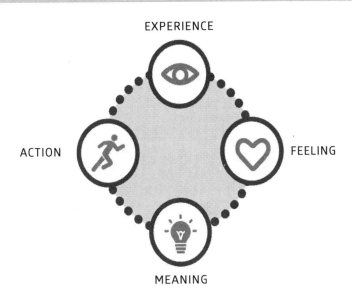

EXPERIENCE

ACTION

FEELING

MEANING

Four questions

1. EXPERIENCE
· What was the key message?
· Rephrase in your own words...
· What did you hear and see?
· What are the cornerstones of..?
· What (just) happened?
· Summarise

2. FEELINGS
· How do you feel about this?
· What was your first emotional reaction?
· Disapointments and surprises?
· Select a cartoon figure that describes your reaction
· Visualizations

3. MEANING
· What does the message mean to you?
· What will change?
· How is this related to your work?
· What is the impact on the ... (individual / team / group)?
· What have we / you learned?
· Why do you think this happened?

4. ACTION
· What will you / we do about this?
· What kind of actions should take place next?
· How are we going to take care of ..
· What could you do better or differently in your work?
· Propose a development area
· What do you need in order to move forward?

Cycle of perception and four questions: Before people can act, they need to create meaning associated with the meeting content.

The Cycle of perception is the theoretical background to the questions that Susanna asked the group after Bert's presentation. According to the cycle of perception, experience, feeling and meaning always take place before action. The cycle's phases run through our minds automatically, but when there's lots of information we don't always have time to examine issues carefully, which can make it can be difficult to reach understanding*.

In order to create understanding and make actions concrete, it helps to ask questions in accordance with the cycle of perception. To do this we first we go through the facts and make sure that the everyone understands the presentation in the same way. Is the experience of the presentation the same for all participants? It is interesting how people can interpret the same information in different ways. For example, people who have just purchased a new car suddenly see the same model everywhere. This perception issue is called frequency illusion, and it can be found in all areas of life, including work. If a person is terrified of losing their job, they may interpret any new information as spelling doom for their career. Therefore, it is important to establish a shared common ground fort the group after a presentation is given. By going through the facts, you can correct any possible misunderstandings and prevent speculation and rumours from taking hold.

Susanna followed Bert's presentation by asking everyone to write down what they viewed as the key points of the presentation on a virtual whiteboard. The whiteboard was shared with everyone, and as people added their input, Susanna and the entire group received instant feedback about how Bert's presentation was understood.

---

*   More about using the questions: The Art of Focused Conversation: 100 Ways to Access Group Wisdom in the Workplace (ICA series) Paperback – April 1, 2000 by R. Brian Stanfield (Editor)

Using the cycle of perception virtually

- **Experience**: Susanna uses a virtual whiteboard where everyone can write down key facts of the presentation. This can later be viewed together as a group or discussed in pairs or small groups.

- **Feelings**: Susanna used a shared slide labeled with an emotional axis. People could place their personal cursor on the axis to match their feelings about the presentation.

- **Meaning**: Small group work where people discuss how the content of the presentation affects their own work and what will change.

- **Action**: Susanna shared a slide with the group which asked, "What will I do and when?" People then provided an answer which Susanna collected to review and then share with everyone else.

Using the cycle of perception virtually; there are many different activities and tools to choose from.

After the facts are established, it is essential to deal with the feelings that have arisen in the group. In situations of change, people are overcome by various emotions and are unable to function normally. Often, just having the chance to share their thoughts and feelings informally can help people to move on. Susanna used a shared slide which had an axis of emotions ranging from very positive to very negative. Each person had their own personal cursor which they placed on the chart depending on their feelings about the presentation.

During the third phase of the cycle of perception, *meaning*, the content of the presentation is pushed further towards action as participants consider the practical meaning of the presentation, such as how their work will be affected by the proposed changes. Susanna broke the large group into smaller groups where people could discuss how the content of the presentation affects their own work. In other words, what does Bert's presentation *mean* to how each individual works? Susanna told each small group to summarize their conversation on their own virtual whiteboard. When everyone re-joined as one large group the whiteboards were shared and the similarities and differences between the conversations were discussed.

The fourth phase of the cycle of perception generates action points based on the facts, emotions, and meaning of the presented content. This phase is the most important, as it helps people plan how the issues in the presentation can be implemented in practice. In the virtual kickoff meeting Susanna used a simple slide where everyone could write down their ideas about what they were going to do next. These are people's individual action points. The virtual software collected each response from the group and Susanna could lay all of the replies on a single chart or a timeline and share it with everyone later.[*]

The cycle of perception always has the same four phases; facts, feelings, meaning, and action. But the questions for each phase can change. The specific question is not what is important. What matters is giving time for participants to reflect and discuss their thoughts about each of the phases of the cycle of perception.

CHECK-OUT

The check-out phase is the finishing touch. During the final phase a common understanding is formed as to why the event was held, its content, and which actions were decided on during the meeting. This phase briefly summarizes the key takeaways from the meeting and it helps participants understand how the meeting went, how new action plans and matters were received, and the companywide mind-set and tone going forward.

---

[*]   This is called *group memory*, and it is a fundamental leadership tool. It is discussed in chapter 4.

The Check-out phase

- Check-out is a meeting practice which allows participants to say something at the end of the meeting.

- In this way, the facilitator helps to create common understanding of the event and decisions made.

- Check-out can also be therapeutic in that you can say what's on your mind or what's bothering you.

- Also efficient for when participants leave mid-meeting. Participants feel better if they can leave feedback or share closing thoughts like the reason for leaving or how successful they think the meeting has or has not been.

In the virtual meeting Susanna simply asked an open-ended question, *how do you feel about the day*, to the group. Then she used a virtual tool that allowed people to 'raise their hand' in the chatroom when they wanted to comment.

Just like the check-in phase of a meeting gets the group warmed-up and ready to participate, the check-out phase of a meeting allows a group to cool down and provides one last opportunity for people to say a few final words, or air any doubts or concerns that they may have. It is infinitely easier to give a presentation or lead a group after the meeting ends if a check-out phase is given.

THE SAME TOOLS BUT DIFFERENT TECHNIQUES

Virtual and face-to-face meetings use the same core tools; the cycle of perception and a clear three-part structure is useful in any meeting environment. In fact, most of the tools that a facilitator uses work in both virtual and face-to-face settings. But to create the best possible virtual meeting environment, Susanna needed to do a few small things differently from how she would run a face-to-face meeting.

Before the virtual meeting, Susanna made sure to spend some time going over the ground rules for her meeting. In most face-to-face meetings, rules such as *be here 100%* are not needed. This is because in face-to-face environments, behaviour is more self-regulating. If a person is in the same room as a presenter, it is much harder to pull out a smart phone and check the day's football scores, or chat with a family member. But in virtual meeting environments, a distraction is just a click away and people can choose to distract themselves without drawing attention. The temptation to use their smartphone is also something that many people cannot resist during virtual meetings. This is why Susanna made sure to begin the virtual meeting by having a slide that presented her ground rules.

Sometimes during a meeting people need to excuse themselves to leave the room or take a phone call. In face-to-face meetings, this is usually done as discreetly as possible, and the meeting leader always knows what is going on because they can see it happening. Virtually, it is a different story and Susanna could easily find herself asking a question to someone who is not even in front of their computer screen. Therefore, she made the ground rule, *be here 100%*. Susanna did not just make this rule to ensure that people were paying attention to her or Bert. Her main concern was people becoming distracted during the group work phase of the meeting. The entire point of the meeting was to get a group to understand and then agree on what actions needed to be taken. The group work phase of the meeting was key in achieving the goals laid out by the kickoff meeting.

She also asked for people to identify themselves by stating their name before speaking to the entire group. In face-to-face meetings this is not needed, as it is obvious who is speaking and when. But no matter how advanced virtual meeting software may be, sometimes it still can be confusing who is talking. By having participants state their name before sharing, it leads to a much better conversational flow that is easier to follow.

One way to structure a face-to-face kickoff meeting

Check-in
- Get people moving and talking in pairs or small groups. Why are we here today?
- Short group discussion; *Why are we here?*

Presentation and reflection
- Presentation
- Individual reflection on the presentation and how it relates to **all four** parts of the cycle of perception. Writing down answers to four questions
- Small group discussion, sharing answers
- Entire group discusses their answers, using the cycle of perception as a guide. You may use a recorder to take notes on a flipchart during this discussion.

Check-out
- A round of comments; *how did the meeting go?*

Check-in

↓

Presentation and reflection

↓

Check-out

Preparing for the virtual meeting was also more time consuming for Susanna. She needed to have a pre-meeting check in phase where everyone tested the technology. The preparation process for face-to-face meetings is usually much easier. All she usually has to do is send out an email with the time and location of the meeting. This is one key difference between the two meeting types; more attention needs to be given to make sure people are comfortable in the virtual environment and that they also can effectively participate in the virtual environment. Think about your working life. How many meetings have you been to? Ten? Fifty? Thousands? Most of them probably have been face-to-face. People know how to attend a face-to-face meeting. They grab a cup of coffee, open a door, and find a seat. But virtual meetings are completely new for many people. Participating in a virtual meeting is not going to feel as natural to most people as a face-to-face meeting does. Susanna needed to prepare everyone for the meeting and give them rules to follow so that they could effectively participate in the virtual environment.

Susanna also needed to adjust how she used the cycle of perception in a virtual environment.

In face-to-face meetings, Susanna would give time for everyone to think about all four aspects of the cycle of perception at once. After giving everyone a few minutes to write down their ideas, she would put people into pairs or small groups where people would talk about the facts, feelings, meaning, and action, all at the same time.

Since virtual meetings are less familiar, Susanna decided to focus on just one aspect of the cycle of perception at a time. This kept the task manageable and simple. If Susanna did not do this, things could have easily become too complex, and people may have become lost in both the content and the technology as they try to click from one slide to another and fill out multiple charts at once.

THE BENEFITS, DISADVANTAGES AND APPLICATION OF A KICKOFF MEETING

Benefits

+ Helps deal with negative emotions. People can't think of concrete action before they have dealt with their negative feelings
+ Using the questions gives participants time to go through issues and discuss them; there will be increased learning and understanding
+ When there is a shared understanding, there will be less gossip and rumors around the office
+ Matters are followed through to action, not left at the discussion stage
+ Ensures immediate feedback on meeting content

Disadvantages

– You need more time-consuming tools to make a concrete implementation plan
– A top-down tool to support communication, or get people to think about the significance of the topic of the presentation in their own activities. Skills and know-how aren't equally combined
– The discussion phase is not meant to produce new ideas

Application

Often, listeners don't understand the content of the presentation they have heard. Four questions based on the cycle of perception is an interactive reflection tool which was created to increase understanding. It can be used to support any presentation. It is particularly useful when presenting a change related to:

· New technology
· Goals
· Way of working
· Merging teams
· Firing or outsourcing
· Values
· Organizational change

After the meeting Susanna is simply brimming with satisfaction. She calls George and excitedly brags to him about her victory.

"It was amazing George. Today I had to run a virtual kickoff meeting where the team was told that the budget was being slashed and the Sales Team's workload was being increased. Not only did I survive the experience without inciting a company-wide riot, the news actually was well received, and everyone was able reflect on what they had heard. They even got to voice their opinions on the matter, and they did so without any shouting, panic, or name calling! It was literally the perfect meeting."

George was happy to hear the good news. "Congratulations! I'm glad that everything went so well, Susanna. I remember being a bit scared before my first virtual meeting. But in the end, I realized that virtual meetings are not that different than standard face-to-face meetings."

Susanna managed to introduce significant changes to the group and then helped everyone process the news and decide together how what actions everyone should take to proceed. And most impressively, she did this virtually. Susanna spends the rest of the evening and a good part of the weekend basking in the glow and positive feelings. She slept soundly that weekend, dreaming of lions attacking tigers, and her Sales Team attacking problems and clearing obstacles.

CHAPTER 3:

THE GOAL IMPLEMENTATION WORKSHOP

Things are going slightly better for Fruit & Loading Inc., and despite the big changes in company policies and uncertain economic conditions, the atmosphere at the workplace is positive.

As the days get shorter and autumn fades into winter, it is time to create an implementation plan for the new goals introduced by Bert. Moreover, these goals are to be implemented before the Christmas apple loading process, which is a very busy time for the company. Susanna finds herself seated in Bert's office, eating an apple Danish pastry. Bert warmly greets her and begins talking.

"You keep proving yourself as a leader, Susanna, and I am impressed. I have personally seen your methods at work in board meetings, and I've been enjoying hearing about the positive reports of your virtual meeting, too. I was a bit worried about what would suffer after putting the travel ban in place, but now I don't think there is any issue that can't be solved with your virtual methods. I am thinking about even opening a virtual therapy business for couples who are thinking of getting a divorce. Think of the marriages we could save!"

Bert waited a moment for Susanna to laugh at his joke and when he realized that she was not going to, he blushed a bit, and continued.

"I want us to use these virtual methods more in the future, but for the next workshop we have a budget set aside that allows for this session to be face-to-face. We are going to hold a goal implementation workshop to make a concrete implementation plan for the new changes. So, this time we are not just communicating strategy, but I want your Sales Team to take part in brainstorming new solutions. You get to facilitate the workshop. How does that sound?"

Susanna immediately thinks of a few new tools she could use to get the group to come up with new ideas and accepts the challenge.

THE GOAL IMPLEMENTATION MEETING

The day of the goal implementation workshop arrives, and Susanna begins the session. With everyone in the room, Susanna goes through the program and begins with an icebreaker activity. She starts by walking around the room and placing a piece of paper on each side of the room with a name of a city written on it. She selected the following four cities that form the compass points of her map; Helsinki, Malaga, Dublin, and Minsk. Susanna thinks that everyone on the Sales Team is from somewhere in Europe or Asia, and that their hometown will fall somewhere within these points.

"If I am not mistaken, everyone here was born somewhere in Europe, which means that your hometown is somewhere on this map. You can see that I have located a few cities that we find on the map. To the north we have Helsinki. Look to the south and we can see Malaga. Towards the east is Minsk and look west and you will see Dublin. These cities form the outline of our map. I want to know where specifically all of you are from, so please stand up and find the place where you were born. Once you have found it, please stand there and raise your hand so I know you are ready."

As the group follows her instructions, Susanna sees that all fifteen participants successfully found their birth places on the map. Rita Barmyfield is from Birmingham, Tony Dingle is from Glasgow, Billy Campbell is from a small village in the Lake District of Finland, and Minna Adams is from Copenhagen. Despite his Germanic-sounding name, Waldemar Wurthenberger is actually from Rome.

Susanna asks participants to find a partner close to them and to share their place of birth. Then she asks participants if they have anything special to share with everyone about their birthplaces. Sales co-ordinator Robson begins to reminisce about the games he used to play in the woods when he was just a whippersnapper. Susanna decides that next time she should make sure to add a clear 'in brief', when she asks people if they have anything to add. Some people really do love to relive old childhood memories.

The map used as a warm-up activity

- The map is a check-in tool for uncovering interesting connections between people.
- In face-to-face workshops first define the area and show locations of at least some cities to help participants orient themselves. Second, invite people to find their spot on the map and to share with the person next to them.

Examples:

MAP OF EUROPE

1. Where you were born
2. Where you've studied
3. Where you have most positive memories
4. Which location would you like to visit

- In virtual meetings ask participants to place their cursor or their name on the map to correspond with the question asked. Once everyone has placed their cursors, ask them to explain their answer.
- Can be used:
  - at the start of a meeting or workshop
  - as an energizer in the middle of a workshop

The map used as a warm-up activity.

Next, Susanna moved on to her next question involving the map. She asked the meeting participants to find the town where they studied. People move around the room and begin to congregate in the university cities of Oxford, Paris and Amsterdam. Susanna notices that Bert is no longer in his birthplace Devon, and she asks him about it.

"Yep, I spent my youth in Devon until I moved to Amsterdam to study."

After finding their locations Susanna asks participants to pair-up and to share their locations again. John explains to Bert, "I studied logistics here in Amsterdam". John and Bert notice that they got their degrees at the same time and from the same place. They even find out that they lived in the same student dormitory! Both marvel at how neither had realized the connection despite having spent more than four years working together. But that's what happens when you concentrate solely on work.

Susanna thanks everyone for the trip down memory lane and tries to get the group to focus on the present. She asks everyone to find the city on the map where they live now and stand there. Apart from one, the group members are all living around Europe.

Minna is not happy. "I live in Tokyo. I can't find my home on this map."

Susanna thanks Minna for coming from so far away and mentions how valuable it is to the company to have everybody present. She remembers to tell the participants how important the warm-up is as it helps the group relax and get to know each other in a new way.

Next, the group writes down its expectations for the workshop and posts their ideas on the wall. Susanna goes through everyone's expectations to make sure everyone is in the right place. Margaret has written something about buying new chairs for the kitchen. Susanna must intervene. "Margaret, you have talked about the chairs for a long time and I know the chairs are important for you, but they are not on the agenda today. You can arrange a meeting with Bert to discuss chairs another time." Margaret sighs and agrees with Susanna. The meeting is off to a great start.

EXPECTATIONS FROM THE GOAL IMPLEMENTATION WORKSHOP..... + your name

Reduce the company expenses – Kevin

Clarify roles and tasks – Rita

Find out what to do with old offices – Billy

Do something new and clarify things a bit – Minna

I want to know what the changes mean in practice – Max

Is there going to be more work – Tina

I want to know what Bert and Susanna think – Alfonso

I am here for a good talk with colleagues – Matt

Just want to have a good talk – Sara

What do we do without office – Sonya

Sort out competitors – John

Give everyone clear directions – Upper-Thrapplewaite

Put a stop to waste – Robson

Haven't got any. I'm quite open-minded. I hope we have some coffee breaks – Tony

The kitchen in the main office needs new chairs – Margaret

To make sure the participants have understood the workshop goals you may ask them to post their expectations on the whiteboard or share via chat in a virtual meeting.

BARRIERS AND SOLUTIONS

Susanna now moves to the heart of the meeting; brainstorming barriers and solutions. "Remember the key goals of the change presented at the kickoff meeting by Bert? They were reducing cost budgets by 50%, increasing customer visits by 25%, and closing the Seville and St. Petersburg offices." Susanna points at three different places in the room where there was a white flipchart with one of the goals written on it.

"Please take a moment to look at the three flipcharts. Each flipchart is going to be the centre of a mini-meeting. There are five spots in each meeting, and you can choose which topic you want to discuss by walking to the meeting place that interests you the most. But when the five spots fill up the meeting is full, you have to choose a different mini-meeting to participate in. Ready? Your task now is to discuss and write down barriers and solutions on the flipcharts for each topic. Get started!"

With the instructions given, Susanna watched as people chose the topic that they wished to discuss. The interest was divided equally, and people divided themselves easily among the three flipcharts, although Tony did seem frustrated that the place discussing cost reductions filled up before he could grab a spot. Thankfully his disappointment was short-lived, and he was soon chatting away with a different group of five.

While monitoring the conversations and fielding any questions that come up, Susanna decides to change groups to continue the discussion. After giving everyone thirty minutes to discuss the topics, she says, "I want to choose group leaders and keep them where they are. Kevin you remain with the group discussion related to cost reduction, and Tony, please stay with the group discussion about the closure of the offices. Margaret, your topic is the increase of sales visits. Everyone else apart from the group leaders will need to switch to a new group. You will spend the next thirty minutes talking about the new topic."

Susanna thought that she gave good enough instructions to make everything clear, but Rita had a question.

"So...you want us to talk about the other topic now...didn't the previous group just do that?! Are we just repeating their ideas?"

"I want you to expand on their ideas. What do you agree with? How did they go wrong? The idea now is for your group to first listen to the team leader explain the ideas and then build off what was said during the first part of the discussion."

After half an hour, she rotates the groups once again, while the team leaders stay put. The 3rd round of discussion is still lively, and the 30 minutes are filled with comments flying back and forth. Susanna must intervene in order to keep the meeting on schedule. "Sorry to interrupt, but your half an hour is up. Would you like an extra fifteen minutes?"

The café method[*]

Stages

1) Choosing topics stage
· 2–4 topics

2) Group work
· divide everyone into groups
  of a similar size
· each group writes down ideas
  and suggestions on the
  flipchart-paper
· If you list barriers first,
  you help people find obstacles
  to reaching the goal and
  solutions get better

3) Rotation
· one member stays with the whiteboard to summarize what was
  discussed as everyone moves between groups
· new groups produce more ideas / comment on the suggestions /
  consider implementation of group's suggestions

4) Prioritising
· have the group priorities the best ideas
· discussion of results

Virtual application of Café method: The best platforms allow
break-out rooms with whiteboards and you can apply the Café
method easily. With other platforms you may have to open many
simultaneous sessions with whiteboards.

Kevin replies, "Yes please", and the conversation continues smoothly for another 15 minutes. After the key solutions and barriers were finished, Susanna asks the participants to prioritise the best ideas by investing ten virtual pounds.

---

[*] The best known Café method is the World Café. You may read more about it: The World Café: Shaping Our Futures Through Conversations That Matter May 15, 2005 by Juanita Brown and David Isaacs

"Alright everyone. In front of all of you are the barriers and solutions for the new goals. I am giving you all ten pounds that are yours to invest in the solutions you think are best. You can either put your whole ten pounds on one idea, split it equally between several, or if you don't like any of the ideas you can keep the money yourself. It's essential that you write the amount you invest clearly next to the solution you choose. That way it will be clear where you put your money."

Kevin interrupted. "Hold on Susanna. Are we just choosing general solutions now, or are we prioritising barriers and challenges, too? Should I invest my ten pounds into the barriers that I think are the most urgent?"

"Good questions Kevin, we used the barriers and challenges to help us think deeper, but at this point we only prioritise solutions. You may choose solutions related to any topic. This is an individual activity, so no talking. Please take around two to three minutes to do this."

Bert cracks a joke. "Robson would probably keep all the money himself, as usual."

The group laughs at Bert's joke and then gets on with the investment task.

Tools to prioritise ideas

Voting techniques
- Give 10 € to best ideas
- Dot-voting
- Traffic light (colour the light)
- Polling

Ranking the ideas
- Give numbers to all ideas

Discussion
- List all ideas and discuss them through; eliminate, improve, group ideas
- Discussion in pairs to allow for more in-depth thoughts/ discussion

There are many different tools a facilitative leader can use to get a group to prioritise ideas.

Susanna was happy with how the meeting was going as she watches the groups prioritise their ideas. *Best of all, they are reaching an agreement! This is no small feat!* Susanna's confidence was high as she thought about how she managed to pull off prioritised solutions. *I still need to turn these ideas into action* she thought, as she addressed the group. "Great job! Now what I want is for the discussion leader from each group to count the points and quickly summarize the key solutions from the conversations that just took place."

The group leaders, Kevin, Margaret and Tony, began summarizing the results. The top choice is better co-ordination of sales leads for increasing the number of customer visits, followed by less travel and making virtual meetings the first step in sales process for reducing costs and, finally, purchasing quality Wi-Fi equipment for everyone to enable working from home for closing the office.

The summaries were clear, and Susanna thought that Kevin, Margaret and Tony did a great job. But she was not done with these discussions just yet.

"The summaries sounded interesting, and I think that there is more that we can squeeze from these topics. But first, let's have a fifteen minutes break."

ACTIONS

After returning from the break, Susanna wants to energise the group by doing something surprising. She enthusiastically informs them, "Stand up and rotate your right leg clock-wise!" Obediently, everyone followed along, and had their right foot in the air, rotating in clock-wise circles.

"Now I want you to stick your right hand out in front of you and draw the number 6 in the air."

Everyone tries to follow Susanna's instructions, and laughter fills the room as everyone's legs begin rotating the opposite direction-counter clockwise.

"You can't draw a 6 with your had while rotating you leg clock-wise. Does anyone know why? It is because the nerves that control your hand and feet are connected, and if you switch the rotational direction of your hand, your foot will follow. Pretty cool, right?" Susanna continues, "You all may have noticed that I sometimes use short and even surprising activities, which don't necessarily have anything to do with the day's agenda. It has been shown that group members can stay awake and focused longer if activities change quickly from tasks related to the agenda to fun games and then back again. This exercise was a good example of such a task. Now, enough silliness, and let's get back to work."

Susanna's energiser called Six-Zero

- In this exercise you ask participants to rotate their right foot clockwise.

- Next you ask everyone to draw a six in the air using their right hand and a top-down movement.

- After this, you explain to the participants that when they do both movements at the same time, the right foot suddenly rotates counter-clockwise by itself.

- When groups try this for the first time, the results are unexpected and hilarious.

- This is a fast energizing exercise, which can be used in groups of all sizes.

"Before us now are the prioritised solutions. Think to yourselves what concrete action you are personally going to take for these solutions. You have three minutes," Susanna announces. She knows that individual thinking can solidify and enhance solutions developed during group discussions and make it easier to come up with answers. However, that is not enough. Action points need to be aligned and developed with colleagues. Susanna adds, "Now form groups of four with the people sitting nearby. Discuss and agree on the best actions that can be taken to make these solutions a reality."

After the groups have had time to think, Susanna points at the big roadmap she has drawn on the wall. "Now we're going to reinforce the actions on this map. Write down the actions in a *who and what* format. Then place them on the timeline in the order in which they should be done. You have ten minutes."

A slide detailing the roadmap to actions. In virtual meetings you may have the participants write their concrete actions on a ready-made roadmap template.

The group writes down their actions successfully. Finally, Susanna asks the participants what they think about the plan. Kevin thinks that the actions are all so brilliant that they don't even need to be prioritised. He shouts, "They are all important and each and every one must be carried out!"

The rest of the group agrees with Kevin.

"What enthusiasm everyone, I am happy to see it. I agree that we do not need to specifically prioritise the actions. They all are important, and they are interdependent. A lot of these actions are not an either-or preposition. What is important is that we follow up on them. I will make sure to email you all a copy of this road map so that we can constantly monitor our progress as we begin to execute the actions listed here."

CHECK-OUT

The clock is fast approaching four. From experience, Susanna knows that the participants are itching to go home. She decided to wrap the day up quickly and on a positive note. A positive feedback ring is next.

"The aim of this ring is to say something positive about each of your colleagues. You have twenty seconds and your time will start when I shout a name. Rita is first!"

"Rita was the most active!"

"She had the best ideas!"

"She's got a really nice voice."

"She has more answers than Google!"

Everyone has something positive to say. The further the feedback ring continues, the wilder the opinions become. Laughter fills the room. Bert is even called 'the fruit king', and Bert himself gives everyone good feedback, which is normally out of character for him. He is a traditional boss who is short on flattery and compliments, even though deep down inside he prefers a soft approach towards leading his troops.

Before the end of the workshop Susanna invites everyone to reflect and give their opinion on the day's session, and not a single person had anything negative to say. The general overall feeling that people expressed about the day was a sense of happiness and accomplishment.

ANALYSIS

On the Saturday following the brainstorming session Bert sends Susanna a text message. "I know you don't have anything better to do. I'll pick you up at twelve."

Susanna wonders what goes on in Bert's mind to make him think that this is normal behaviour, but she decides to text him back, saying that she will be ready and waiting. At twelve precisely, the doorbell rings. Susanna is relieved to see a wide smile on Bert's face.

"I thought I'd surprise you. Hop in!"

A shiny new sports car is parked outside Susanna's door.

"A new car? For me? As a token of your appreciation for all I have done? I don't know what to say, thanks Bert!" exclaims Susanna, not entirely believing her own words.

Bert laughs deeply. "You have done an outstanding job recently Susanna, that is undeniable. But you are a crazy person if you think this car is for you. It's mine of course. Now get in and let's get going."

Susana complies, and a few minutes later the colleagues whizz through the busy city centre. After a while, Bert begins to tell Susanna what is on his mind.

"I'm quite surprised by the goal implementation workshop. I never recognized what an idea bank we have among the team. We were able to get refined results from suggestions with the entire team there. If we can get everyone to work together, we can come up with all kinds of new ideas for Fruit & Loading Inc.'s future. Expansion, growth, new fruit loading and transportation methods...we could even expand on to other kinds of fruit. Like the new red Christmas pear, that could be our future..."

Bert continues on about Christmas pears and other exotic fruits for half an hour without stopping. Susanna notices a new kind of enthusiasm in her boss. Something important must have fallen into place during the goal implementation workshop. It seemed that Bert was inspired by the team and how they helped shape the future of Fruit & Loading Inc.

Bert kept talking. "The meeting went well, but would it have worked as successfully in a virtual setting?"

"Yes, I think so. Small details would need to be changed, but the important stuff is kept the same. In a face-to-face workshop we used flipchart paper and markers. In virtual meetings everyone is using his/her keyboard and writing on the whiteboard. The result is more or less the same. The principles of working are the same. However, the technology still makes me nervous, there is always someone's computer running out of battery or microphone not working."

Susanna followed an important principle in her workshop; all phases of the workshop involved both divergent and convergent thinking. This meant that there was time for both brainstorming and idea selection in each part of the workshop. Renowned psychologist J.P. Guildford suggested in the 1950s that creative thinking can be divided into these two very different phases.

Divergent thinking is necessary for producing new ideas, while convergent thinking is needed when evaluating the usefulness of new ideas. Both methods of thought are needed to achieve productive creativity, and that's what brainstorming is at its best; creative work fueled by everyone's skills, history, emotions and abilities. The facilitator's core task is to bring forth the group's ideas (divergence) and help the group to select the best ones (convergence). The easiest way to list ideas is to collect them on a flipchart paper or virtual whiteboard and choose the best ones.

Divergent thinking – creation of new ideas

Convergent thinking – logical analysis and selection of best ideas

Divergent and convergent thinking: both need to be accounted for when planning a workshop.

In a typical workshop divergence and convergence is repeated three times. The stages of the workshop correspond to the three-phase process that has been the structure of other meetings and workshops that Susanna has led; clarifying, solutions, and action. First, the problem or target is clarified. After this, solutions to the problems or targets are found, and finally they are made real by transforming them into actions. This is done by thinking of the steps needed to act on the solutions. These steps should be presented in a *who, what, and when* format. These core stages come between the check in stage which prepares everyone for the session, and the check-out stage, which gives closure to the group and summarizes the results of the clarifying, solutions, and action stages. This format works especially well for solving problems and for leading various development workshops.

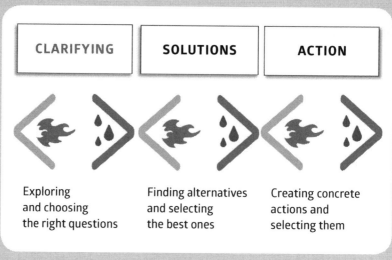

| CLARIFYING | SOLUTIONS | ACTION |

Exploring and choosing the right questions

Finding alternatives and selecting the best ones

Creating concrete actions and selecting them

Key stages of a typical workshop; Clarifying, Solutions, Action.

However, in her goal implementation workshop Susanna followed a slightly different path; goals did not need to be clarified simply because the goals had been already chosen by Bert. Also, the goals did not need long introductions because they had already been introduced at the kickoff meeting.

Bert rouses Susanna from her daydream by saying, "So what was this rotation thing you did once you had introduced the goals?"

"I set up a café. I started the traditional way by dividing everyone up into groups. After that, I rotated the groups. One participant always stayed to explain the ideas."

"Wow that was simple and effective. I'd never thought of rotating the groups. We had a fantastic talk in the small groups about different solutions and we had time to explore each other's ideas in depth."

"There were only three groups, so it was quite easy to coordinate them, and everything went fine when they went over the solutions. Next time, I'm going to try to do the same virtually!" Susanna laughs, while savouring her wine.

Bert still wants to know how Susanna managed to finish up the workshop.

The structure of Susanna's goal implementation workshop

Check-in
- Susanna introduces workshop goals and program.
- Susanna shows a map of Europe and has people find their hometowns and places of study. This gets people chatting and comfortable. It's also fun!
- Susanna focuses the participants by asking them to write and post expectations.

Clarifying
- Susanna re-introduces the goals deployed in the previous meeting.

Barriers and Solutions
- Susanna begins using the Café method. She makes three meetings; one for each aspect of the goal. In each meeting barriers and solutions are generated. Participants rotate between topics and someone always stays to explain. Finally solutions are prioritised.
- Susanna calls the entire group together and the prioritised solutions are summarised.

Break

Action
- Susanna uses a visual roadmap to get action points for each prioritised solution.
- Participants write down actions, share and align them in small groups and post actions on the roadmap.
- Susanna calls the entire group together to discuss and evaluate the work.

Check-out
- Positive feedback ring: Susanna asks the group to say something positive about each participant for 20 seconds.
- Final questions/comments/feedback

"I used a virtual roadmap. The participants marked the actions on the road at suitable intervals for implementation. As usual with this method, actions which can either be implemented immediately, in a couple of weeks or in several months were placed on the roadmap," Susanna reminds her friend.

Bert adds, "You could probably divide the roadmap into shorter or longer timelines depending on the topic. The roadmap is a brilliant tool for condensing actions, and it's easy to monitor."

Susanna thanks Bert for the kind words and asks Bert what he thought about the positive feedback exercise which resulted in some outrageous compliments being thrown around.

"That was brilliant. It gave a very positive flavour to the whole workshop. And it was the first time I received positive feedback in this company since I opened the front door for Margaret three years ago!"

Susanna laughed and explained her reasoning for choosing this activity. "I was actually a bit nervous regarding the activity. A facilitator would never want to use the positive feedback loop in a session where tensions are high, or morale is low. If you did, some rude things could be said, or even worse, nothing would be said at all! Our session dealt with some difficult topics; closing an office, increasing sales, cutting costs... I would not have dared to try it if the general mood had been negative, but I read the group as feeling positive and upbeat about the solutions they thought of, and the exercise ended up being a great fit."

Bert nodded, and said, "the mood was positive, but only because we had communicated the changes beforehand in the kickoff meeting and dealt with negative emotions. That prepared the team for the next step and allowed them to move forward."

THE BENEFITS AND DISADVANTAGES OF GOAL IMPLEMENTATION WORKSHOPS

Benefits
· Helps create understanding of goals
· With understanding comes the ability to self-organise
· Helps to deal with barriers
· Enables people to align their activities
· Increases commitment and responsibility

Disadvantages
· Empowering the group always means less control for leader

Susanna smiled. The goal implementation workshop was another success, and they managed to create goals based around negative news like reduced budgets, or office closures. Goal implementation workshops focus the team on goals and helps team members align their actions. It is a key activity when creating high performance teams. Susanna was even able to take things a step further and help the team create concrete actions based on achieving these goals. This was a big step for her in her career as a facilitator, and she had good reason to smile.

Unfortunately, not everyone in Fruit & Loading Inc. was relaxing and feeling as content as Susanna was. A member of Susanna's Sales Team was angrily cursing Bert and Susanna's names. This employee was not happy about some of the changes announced. Susanna had no way of knowing this at the time, but she was soon going to find out and face this challenge head-on.

Situations for applying
the goal implementation workshop

Susanna's goal implementation workshop is a tool for making a concrete action plans for any goals related to:

· New technology

· Performance, financial, learning, growth goals

· Way of working

· Merging teams

· Values

· Organisational change

CHAPTER 4:

SUPPORTING GOAL IMPLEMENTATION WITH COACHING

A week after the successful goal implementation workshop, Susanna is at home, sitting comfortably in her favourite chair. Her mind wanders to work related matters.

After Bert's presentation I felt happy. Generally, the changes had been accepted by the team and everyone seemed willing to adapt and make these changes work, instead of fighting them. But how can we follow through on the action plan....this part worries me. Is anyone even doing anything now to continue the momentum we have built?

Susanna decided to have personal follow-up meetings with each team member in response to all the changes that the company has recently gone through. But as Susanna thought about the annual development meetings, she realised that the meetings could have a good purpose in theory, but in practise they often were negative and counterproductive.

It seems like the development discussions have a negative feeling before they even being. People arrive with the idea that I will just criticize their work. If I have something to say about their performance, I try to say it constructively, but giving feedback often leads to arguing, or people disengaging and shutting down.

Susanna was thinking about the new Coaching skills she had recently learned. *This time it was going to be different.*

Susanna opens her laptop and begins typing out the invitation for coaching sessions.

To my beloved Sales Team,

Following Bert's announcement of new strategic goals, I would like to have a coaching session with each team member to make sure we get the new goals implemented. The recent travel ban means that the sessions will be held virtually for everyone located outside of London. Soon you will each receive an invitation to a virtual meeting. Please make sure you reviewed the memo from the previous workshop and have answered the questions in the attached form before the event. I really want all of us to spend some time thinking over the questions so that we can have the most productive meeting possible.

Best Regards,
Suzy

The first meeting was scheduled with Matthew Stevens. Matthew was a sharp salesman and very successful at his job. However, he seemed to enjoy arguing over the smallest of details. She was not expecting an easy discussion. Last year when she had her development discussion with Matthew, there was a bit of tension in the room. Matthew flat out said that he was underpaid, and that some of the requirements put on the Sales Team were at odds directly with the ultimate goal of company well-being. This was where Susanna's mind was as she made small talk with Matthew after he had clocked in to the virtual meeting room.

After talking about the weather and Matthew's fishing trip to Northern Siberia, Susanna introduces the format of the meeting. "First, we will upload your answers to the questions I sent in the invitation email, and you will have a chance to explain your replies and I will keep a record of all new ideas or changes to your original plan. Generally, I welcome ideas from you and the rest of the team, and I love hearing about all of them. I want all of them to become a reality. However, I have to keep the budgets and sales-targets in mind and I may have to set some constraints. Does that sound fair?"

Matthew replied, "Susanna, you always set some constraints, but I like the fact that you explain the logic that you use. This format seems OK with me."

The discussion started well. But when Matthew and Susanna came to Matthew's proposed sales targets for next year, Susanna noticed a decrease in the number of customer visits and increase in the sales volume. "Matthew, you are planning to sell more next year while decreasing the number of your customer visits. Also, you do remember that just a week ago it was announced that the required number of sales visits increased by 25%. Could you explain this to me?"

"It is not the number of visits, but instead the quality of the visits that counts. I won't be visiting the smaller customers next year, I will just deal with them virtually. Instead, I will focus all of my travel on visiting the bigger clients. I will have fewer customer visits overall, but I will be actually visiting the larger customers more than I do now."

"And you think that will bring us better results?" asked Susanna.

"Absolutely. The Novosibirsk market in Russia actually has only twenty major fruit distributors. They are difficult and demanding clients, but they also control 90% of the market. If I concentrate on the smaller distributors, then that will be an economic disaster for the customers".

"Matthew, what are you actually planning to do?"

"I am going to visit the major customers once a month. I will hang out in their offices and get to know the people very well. That will mean one visit every other day of the month. That, along with all the office work, will be more than enough to fill my time."

Matthew was making a passionate argument for his ideas, but Susanna was not quite convinced. She believed that Matthew had valid points when coming up with this plan, but she didn't completely follow all of his logic behind it. And most of all, she feared that by doing something completely different from what Bert had just implemented would be considered disrespectful to Bert's authority. She thought for a moment and said, "I appreciate your suggestion and it makes sense, but it goes directly against what Bert has just announced. What about the new target for customer visits? The 25% increase? He already thinks the salesmen spend far too much time in the office. You may need to reconsider your plan."

"Sure, I can do that," Matthew says furiously. "But Bert is crazy and simply wrong. His strategy will not bring the desired results. At least not with my current customers."

Susanna stopped Matthew. "Matt, calm down. I'm not asking you to be happy about Bert's new strategy, but you need to remain respectful. There are better ways to communicate than being angry and passive-aggressive."

"Hold on Susanna! I'm not being disrespectful. All I am trying to do is explain why I think my idea is better..."

Matthew continued to explain his plan of visiting customers. Susanna listened to his voice through the internet as he detailed his plan to her and she thought that Matthew was not being rude after all.

A few more minutes passed, and Matthew was finished with his lengthy monologue. Susanna thought about his ideas for a bit and decided to let Matthew follow his instincts. "OK Matthew, I get your point. If you increase your sales I will make sure that you don't have to increase the number of customer visits. But we are going to have to track your results closely. Is there any way that I could support your work?"

"Of course I will increase my sales, but I know that when the sales activity reports are published next month with mine showing a decrease in customer visits Bert is going to give me a kick in the butt. Could you somehow break the news to him and explain to him why?"

"Fine, I'll talk to Bert. I think I can explain this somehow."

The rest of the discussion went smoothly, and Susanna and Matthew were able to easily agree on concrete actions. When it came time for the meeting to end, Matthew shared his feelings on the process and the current state of communication within the company.

"The discussion was easy because I already understood the big picture after Bert's presentation. Also, the discussion seems to be easier when you have key ideas recorded on the computer screen," commented Matthew when checking out from the meeting. Susanna could not help but to agree.

After meeting with Matthew, Susanna wanted to improve the following virtual coaching session. The next day, Susanna had a meeting scheduled with Beth, another member of the Sales Team. Beth's voice, like Matthew's, was robotic and a bit distorted by the virtual meeting software, but something was different.

"I love your new haircut Susanna" squealed Beth, as the meeting was about to begin. This meeting was also a virtual one, but Susanna and Beth were looking at one another and smiling. Susanna had decided to try and use video app of her meeting software to improve communication during virtual meetings, and so far, it appeared to be working. Susanna did not want to use the video conferencing software for the whole meeting, in fact, this was not possible because she wanted to have her questions visible to keep focus and she was recording key points on the whiteboard. She decided to use video app during the check-in, and check-out phases. As Susanna led the meeting, she thought that the conversation felt more natural. A connection was made during the check-in phase of the meeting when the two women were smiling and Beth complimented Susanna on her haircut. This connection then carried over to the rest of the meeting.

The meeting lasted over an hour, and the combination of Susanna's idea to use video, along with an extremely extroverted Beth, led for many thoughts to be shared about Bert's new sales targets and client visitation schedule. Susanna glanced at her watch and realized that it was time to wrap up the meeting.

"Beth, I think now is a good time to wrap up the meeting. But before we do, I want you to help me summarize the key points of today's meeting. What are your most important thoughts and actions based on what was discussed today?"

"That's easy, Susanna. I have two things that perfectly summarize our meeting. First, I will need to reach out to potential new clients in order to build up a relationship strong enough for a visit with them to feel natural and go well. Second, I am going to talk with some of the other Sales Team members and try to get some tips about how to ensure a good client visit. I am friends with most of the clients I visit now, and those visits are easy. But I want to get stronger and more confident for my new visits."

All in all, Susanna was pleased with the meeting; Beth had a lot to say, Susanna's idea to use video during the check-in and check-out phases of the meeting helped create a comfortable and relaxed meeting environment.

Susanna's meeting with Dave was a bit different than the rest. Dave's sales district was central London, which meant that he lived in the city, and often worked in the same office building as Susanna. This meant that they could have the meeting in person.

I forgot how nice it is to have a meeting in person once in a while, thought Susanna while she listened to Dave talk. The virtual coaching sessions had been a success but now the conversation was flowing even better, and she could see that Dave was engaged.

Dave's key concern in response to Bert's new strategy was how to maintain quality *and* meet the new targets.

Susanna liked this thought a lot, and she thought that while people had to adjust in order to meet Bert's new targets, the outstanding work that they already are doing could not suffer. So, she picked up a pen and wrote down in large letters on the whiteboard, 'Maintain quality AND meet new goals.'

As she wrote this down, Susanna realized that she had picked a new habit from her virtual meetings.

The flipchart! I am recording all key points on the flipchart for both of us to see. Dave can stay better focused on the meeting and in the end we can review this to make action points, summarize...get feedback...

"Don't mind me Dave, please keep sharing your ideas. I will be here writing down the key points so that we can review them later."

Susanna kept writing as Dave kept talking. As she wrote down the main points, she noticed how he then quickly came up with another opinion.

The discussion at the end of their meeting was a success too. With the flipchart filled with notes from their meeting, Dave and Susanna had all the information they needed to have a meaningful conversation about the new strategy and how it affected Dave. With all of the information written on the wall and available to use as a reference point, it was easy for Dave to maintain focus when he was trying to come up with his action points. Susanna noticed that Dave's solutions and actions made sense because they factored in much more information than if Susanna did not write and display the meeting notes.

After the meeting had ended, Susanna decided that she would be recording meetings as much as she could; if her meeting with Dave was any indicator, it was an important task.

ANALYSIS

This is a book on leading groups – not individuals. Nevertheless, we have added a chapter on coaching which is not a group activity. If I had to choose one activity to follow-up group performance, I would choose the progress meeting that will be introduced in chapter 10. In a progress meeting the leader helps participants to see the full picture, to exercise their initiative and to coordinate their actions. Coaching helps people think more clearly and it is a powerful tool in focusing people on goals and boosting individual performance.

The main purpose of coaching is to clarify the goals and to make actions concrete. In addition, coaching helps find the potential of each team member. When abilities are defined and a plan of how to proceed is outlined, expectations of future behavior are set, both for the team leader and the employee.

Coaching was an important leadership tool for Susanna. It was vital to her that these discussions were constructive and motivating. She made the sessions as participatory as possible in order to create maximum commitment. That is why she was using her coaching skills instead of just giving instructions and answers to the team members. Before Susanna held even one coaching session, she sent a list of key questions and areas for thought to her team. This way, the conversation would be two-sided, and the Sales Team members would be prepared to chat with Susanna, instead of just arriving to the meeting ready to listen.

A coaching leader helps the employee find answers by asking questions. The questions provoke thought and because employees find the answers themselves instead of being taught, the coaching sessions creates better motivation. When coaching, the key tool used by the coach are questions about business and personal development goals, the current challenges of the employee, solutions, and then actions.

The structure of Susanna's coaching session

Pre-work
· Susanna sends the questions in advance

Check-in
· A little small talk
· Susanna introduces coaching goals, her role and the steps

Clarifying
· What is your concrete business and personal development goal?
· When you imagine a successful end of the year, what have you accomplished?

Solutions
· What is stopping you?
· What are the solutions?
· Which solutions should be implemented?

Action
· What are you going to do and when?
· What kind of support do you need in order to succeed?

Check-out
· How did it go?

But Susanna was not coaching all the time. She definitely did not want her team to decide for themselves what they wanted to do, even though this approach might have resulted in the best commitment. As team leader, Susanna also wanted to influence the discussion herself. She was not going to let a single suggestion be implemented without her consent. She was looking for a good discussion leading to mutual agreement. That is why she first wanted everyone to suggest and explain their ideas. Next, she explained her viewpoint and commitment to the ideas which lead to the end result of developing a common agreement on issues.

There are potential difficulties in Susanna's approach. What if the employee suggests an idea and then Susanna rejects the idea? This could make the employee feel angry and disrespected. There are many solutions to this problem. The first principle is to show appreciation and understanding for all ideas. Next, it is important to talk about possible constraints and then give the question back to the employee. For instance, "Matthew, I understand that you want to attend a training course. We do not have a budget for that this year. Could you think of any other ways of learning sales skills?"

What to do with a suggestion

· Accept the idea
· Give thanks and show appreciation for the idea
· Prioritise
· Say no when you have to
· Suggest another solution
· Give the idea back with constraints for further reflection and development
· In the end, express your commitment to agreed actions

If you must turn down an employee's idea, you can leave the door open for further ideas to be shared if you accept and show appreciation for the proposed idea.

Susanna took notes during her meetings, which she then displayed in the meeting room. This practice is a facilitation tool called *group memory*. Group memory is a visual record of the meeting, and it helps maintain the focus of a group. When Susanna began using this tool in her meetings, she achieved several benefits. She eliminated the problem of lost content, and the use of group memory also greatly improved the quality of discussion in the meetings. In general, people are typically only able to work with one idea at a time. Group memory is an extension of the brain and it allows the mind to compare and work on many ideas simultaneously. Anything more than one idea, and details become hazy and the content suffers. The human memory is also very short, and meetings are usually filled with new information. Without group memory, it is a struggle to remember the content. Group memory works as an extension of the brain; all important points are catalogued and on display for future reference, which allows for an enriched, more complex analysis and discussion.

In larger meetings, *group memory* helps new ideas to become accepted by a larger group. The meeting leader does not write down who said what when taking notes, just the key points. This way, an idea or thought loses ownership when it is recorded. Later on, when the group refers back to the recorded *group memory*, the content is there, together. Specific ideas lose ownership, and instead become shared group property.

In her meeting with Dave, Susanna tried her best to identify the key points of the conversation and then write them down on the whiteboard for Dave and her to refer to. When it came time for Dave to think up action points, he did so using the information that Susanna had written down. This naturally resulted in actions and solutions that were based on a complete understanding of the problem. When *group memory* is not used, it is harder to think of logical solutions and actions as logic naturally suffers as information is not accounted for or forgotten.

Group Memory is an important tool, and it should be a constant feature in both virtual and face-to-face meetings. The most effective way for a meeting leader to use group memory is to just write down the key points of a meeting as they are said, either on a flipchart, or in a virtual whiteboard. If you use a flipchart, fill up one page, tape it to the wall and then begin filling up the next page. This way, everyone will be able to see all the notes from the meeting at one time, and they will be able to easily jump from one page to another, as they use this valuable 'extension of the brain'.

The importance of group memory

Group memory is a visual record of the meeting that supports common focus.

Human memory is very short. Meetings are full of (new) information. Without a group memory people will quickly forget what has been said.

Group memory creates investment in new ideas. When written on group memory without the inventor's name, ideas quickly became shared property. This supports commitment, decision making and implementation.

Seeing all information displayed on Group memory ensures that the solutions and actions match the initial topic.

A great tool which is easy to use: in face to face meetings, the facilitator writes down key points and takes notes on a flipchart. In virtual meetings the facilitator can take notes on a whiteboard.

Susanna's coaching sessions were a success. She listed to the ideas and input of her employees, which increased their commitment to follow their outlined strategic actions. Susanna was also adaptable in her own methods, willing to acknowledge the shortcomings of her meetings as they appeared and then make changes to fix them. All in all, she was pleased by the results of the coaching sessions. But everything wasn't sunshine and roses in Susanna's world. After all, every action has an equal and opposite reaction and allowing Matthew to ignore the new policy and follow his own ideas meant that the vision of her boss was being directly ignored. This would cause big problems which came in the form of a furious Bert.

THE BENEFITS, CHALLENGES, AND APPLICATION OF COACHING

Benefits
· Helps employees reflect and understand
· Empowers and creates commitment
· Furthers the alignment of activities

Challenges
· If the leader already has answers and solutions, coaching is not the right tool

Application
· Supports goal attainment in any situation

CHAPTER 5:

THE PROBLEM SOLVING WORKSHOP

After the individual coaching sessions with her Sales Team, Susanna was optimistic about how things were going. People were enthusiastically coming up with ideas about how to adapt to the new strategic plan, and some, like Matthew, thought that they had even better ideas than the plan itself! After thinking things over, Susanna was even beginning to come around to Matthew's new plan, which called for less overall sales visits to customers, but more time given to large customers. She was grateful that meaningful ideas were coming from the bottom up, and not just being handed down by Bert and herself.

Speaking of Bert, he was furious! And it was with an angry Bert who Susanna found herself on the phone speaking to, struggling to get a word in between his turbulent outbursts.

"We have a new sales strategy and you've told Matthew that he does not have to implement it...What are the other salesmen going to say!? The whole strategy does not seem credible anymore. You have completely undermined my power and ability to lead the organization if people realize that they do not have to follow the plans I JUST DECIDED ON! Just tell me, what were you thinking? Is this some sort of ill-conceived revenge plot you are unleashing on me?"

Despite herself, Susanna forced back a giggle at Bert's overdramatic words and replied, "Just hear me out Bert, I assure you that-"

"No, no, and NO! Susanna, you are going to force Matthew to follow the new strategy!"

"OK Bert, sure I will. But Matthew really had a point," Susanna countered.

"If you have a point you must have evidence. Where is your evidence? This is just an attempt by Matthew to reduce his workload. That's the beginning and the end of it," Bert spat.

Susanna gave Bert a moment to cool down, and asked, "Well shouldn't we hear Matthew out and maybe give him a chance to explain why he thinks this is a good idea?"

Bert was quiet. Although he sometimes is quick to get angry, Susanna knew that he was reasonable at heart and would agree that hearing Matthew out would be the best course of action. Sure enough, after a moment of sulking, he seconded Susanna's suggestion.

"Susanna, we are lifting the travel ban for just this one meeting with Matthew. Make arrangements for him to be in the London office as soon as possible so that the three of us can have a problem solving session about this."

Susanna did as she was told, and the meeting was scheduled. Susanna was not the type who loved conflict, so she was not really looking forward to facilitating a problem solving meeting between an angry Bert and a stubborn Matthew. However, she knew that a well-structured plan is the key towards successful meetings, and she already spent the night before developing a plan for this meeting. She felt confident as she said hello to Bert and Matthew as they walked into the small conference room. As Susanna settled in to start the meeting, she could feel the tension between Bert and Matthew. Bert was peering over his cup of coffee, looking at Matthew. Matthew, not intimidated, was trying to play it cool, idly twirling his fingers. Susanna did her best not to let any of this get her down.

"Welcome to our problem solving meeting," started Susanna. "You have both expressed interesting ideas on how to increase sales. I know that you both are excited about your own ideas, and you think that your specific idea is the solution needed to increase sales. I've invited you both here to really find out what is hindering our sales. The purpose of this meeting is to find out the core issues that are stopping us from selling more. Could you kindly both tell me what you think about the agenda?"

"I'm interested by what will be said. Let's begin right away," said Bert quickly.

Matthew on the other hand was not as eager to begin. "I am a bit worried about sharing ideas in front of both of my bosses, especially if my ideas go directly against yours. I am not usually a religious man, but I can tell you right now I am praying to God that you don't hold any of this against me. Part of me is saying to keep my mouth shut, but I have gone against my better judgement so far, and there is no turning back now."

Bert and Susanna both assured Matthew that being open and speaking his mind is the best course of action, and they began the meeting.

"Let's first define the symptoms of the problem," suggested Susanna. "We are all worried about the sales, right?"

"Yes, our sales are inadequate, and we need to increase sales in order to survive," replied Bert.

Hearing this, Susanna picked up a pen and drew a circle on the right side of the whiteboard that was located at the front of the room. She filled the inside of the circle with the words 'inadequate sales'.

Susanna continued, "OK, now let's try to logically decide what is causing these poor sales until we identify the root cause. Does anyone have an idea what is causing the problem?"

Bert answered with, "Sales volume is a clear function of the number of visits by our Sales Team. Too few customer visits on the part of our Sales Team is clearly the cause. If they visit customers more, sales would increase."

"OK. What is causing the low number of visits?", asked Susanna, attempting to moderate this discussion.

"An unmotivated Sales Team!" shouted Bert, while Matthew meekly interjected, "...And lack of time."

"And what causes these effects?" posed Susanna.

Bert continued loudly, "Salesmen are not motivated because they are not properly managed. They need to be pushed and motivated."

Susanna stopped Bert. "Bert, you do not need to come up with solutions yet. First we need to identify and choose the problems we want to solve."

Matthew continued, "I have a cause for the lack of time. Salesmen are busy with taking routine orders at the office. And that problem is due to the lack of proper working processes and roles. And that in turn is due to management's ignorance of work processes which is due to management's arrogant attitude towards details."

Susanna held her breath as she waited for Bert to explode in response to Matthew's bold comments, but Bert surprised Susanna and Matthew both by immediately saying, "The management is out of touch. I guess we really do not understand what is happening."

Bert's unexpected comment was followed by a long silence. The meeting was getting truly interesting, and perhaps a bit dangerous too. Susanna decided to press forward with her questions.

"Can anyone find a cause for management's attitude? No? Then we must be getting close to the root cause. Let's start from the beginning. Does anyone have another idea on what causes inadequate sales?"

"Sure", said Matthew. "The salesmen are wasting their time with the wrong customers, and that is caused by the lack of categorization of customers. Some customers only place one small order each quarter, while others spend millions and purchase whole fruit orchards at a time. But for some crazy reason, we allocate both customers the same amount of time. How does this make sense?"

The discussion carried on as Susanna led the group in a root cause analysis exercise to explore causes of inadequate sales until they began to feel the picture is complete. After Susanna felt that enough root causes were thought of, it was time to select the most relevant ones to change.

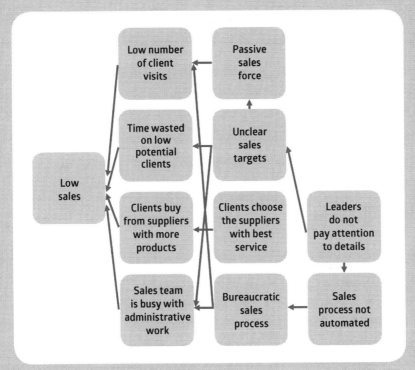

The current reality tree for Bert, Matthew and Susanna. Current reality trees are part of the technique called Root Cause Analysis.

"Now let's choose the causes that have the highest impact on inadequate sales and that we can actually influence," instructs Susanna.

As usual, Bert begins with his ideas. "I would like to choose the arrogant attitude of the management towards details, however I think that this has already began to change for the better during this meeting. I think we should at least solve the problems with customer categorization and sales processes. What do you think Matt?"

Matthew agrees, and Susanna keeps writing down more and more key issues as Bert and Matthew continue talking. Finally, she guides them to the next portion of the meeting. "Guys are you ready to brainstorm solutions?"

"I think the first solutions are clear," claims Matthew. "We have to start categorizing customers and create a new system for taking routine orders."

"I agree completely that we need to be separating larger clients from smaller ones. It is a bit ridiculous that we do not even have more specific labels besides 'retail client', 'business client', or 'international client.' I also agree about a new order system. I have seen some suppliers automate regular orders. This way, it uses the smallest possible amount of company resources. We need to automate what we can in order to use less of the Sales Team's time."

Bert and Matthew kept discussing the pros and cons of different solutions, all while Susanna kept taking notes on a flipchart; *group memory* was an important part of all the meetings that Susanna led.

After a few more moments of discussion, Bert is shocked at how they arrived to the solutions. "After we chatted about the issues it seems that solutions just popped-up naturally. It is interesting that when you think about problems the solutions become clear. We could brainstorm how to do the categorization or what kind of system we should have for taking orders, but I feel tired now. And perhaps we need to gather some data. Let's deal with the details of these solutions later."

Susanna led them on to the next phase of the meeting. "Alright gentlemen, before we end the meeting take a look at the whiteboard with all of the solutions listed on it. Keeping these in mind, what should your next actions be? What will you do to make sure that these solutions become a reality? Bert? Matthew?"

"Based on my experience with clients I could make a proposal on how to categorize customers," suggested Matthew.

Bert nodded in agreement. "Nice one Matthew. I would be very interested in seeing what you come up with. I am going to prove the change of my arrogant attitude by getting some sales data to support our findings for the need for categorization. Then I am going to put my data together with Matthew's practical findings and we will create a new client categorization system. Also, I will get the IT guys to develop a new system for receiving orders. Finally, I will talk to the Management Team. Other teams may be experiencing similar issues that we have talked about here. I will try and help them learn from our problems, and how we solved them today."

"And if at this point you do not mind me stepping out of the facilitator role, I will work closely with the IT guys to ensure that their solutions will be practical," added Susanna, as she finished writing down all of the actions points that the group had just discussed. "I am going to take some pictures of all of the notes on the flipchart, so you both will have a record of everything that was said today. I also will make a slide with all our actions on it listed together. I will send it to you so that we have something concrete that we can follow up on in the upcoming weeks. And finally, I will call a follow-up meeting in three weeks to see how we are advancing with all our actions."

It was time for the check-out phase, and Susanna asked Matthew and Bert how they felt the meeting went.

"I had no reason to worry about this meeting. I think we got really good results," said a relieved Matthew. Bert and Susanna agreed and wished him well as he left the meeting room to get back to work.

After Matthew had gone, Bert and Susanna remained behind.

"This was a great experience. Matthew proved himself right and he would make a better Director than myself. But I will never admit this fact to him or anyone else," thought Bert out loud.

"I think you are a good Director Bert because you know when to listen. And sometimes Matt is OK too," finished Susanna. You could hear from her voice that she was pleased with how things went.

ANALYSIS

Problem solving meetings often involve conflict. This makes them one of the most difficult types of meetings to lead. When emotions become involved, rationality and level-headedness sometimes leave us. This is completely natural, but to combat this, problem solving meetings always need to have a strong structure and outline that the meeting leader can fall back on if emotions run high. Susanna knew this, and she used the following meeting structure for her problem solving meeting.

She first began with the check-in phase, which allowed Bert and Matthew to get comfortable and discuss the meeting agenda. During the check-in phase Matthew voiced his concern about speaking his mind so directly to his bosses. Bert and Susanna were able to give him reassurance that being truthful and conflictual is better than biting your tongue and following along with something that you do not have faith in or agree with.

The check-in phase is especially important in problem solving meetings as it sometimes diffuses some tension felt between parties, and at least allows all participants to negotiate and agree upon the meeting agenda. This may not seem like a huge agreement that is being reached, but it starts the meeting off on the right foot and can set a collaborative tone for the rest of the meeting.

The next step in Susanna's problem solving meeting was defining the actual problem. This is not just naming the conflict but using a higher-level tool to look past symptoms and analytically specify the problem at hand. For this, Susanna uses a tool called root cause analysis.

The structure of Susanna's face-to-face problem solving meeting

Check-in
· Susanna leads small group discussion about the meeting agenda and any concerns or questions about the meeting.

Clarifying the problem
· Root cause analysis is used to identify the underlying causes of the issue 'inadequate sales' and key problems are chosen.

Solutions
· Group discussion led by Susanna. Susanna uses group memory and takes notes during this discussion.

Action
· Bert, Matthew and Susanna think about their best actions to follow achieve the solutions. Susanna writes these actions down on a flipchart and she will send them to Bert and Matthew later as a plan that the three can follow.

Check-out
· Susanna asks Matthew and Bert for feedback about how the meeting went.

After the problem is defined, meeting participants create solutions and action plans for these problems in the following two stages of the problem solving meeting; the solutions and the action stages. The solutions stage is a time for brainstorming. It is here where ideas about how to fix the outlined problems can be thrown around in a safe environment. The action stage then requires meeting members to concretely state what they specifically will do next to act on the solutions. A general statement such as, "I will try to be a better listener" does not cut it in this phase. Specific, detail-oriented steps are needed. A better statement for the action stage would be, "By the end of the year, I will read the book, *Listening: The Forgotten Skill* by M. Burley-Allen, and take a business communications class at the city's business college." These are steps that can be tracked and that lead to change, instead of a vague, broad statement.

Then the meeting ends with a check-out stage which consists of discussion about what happened during the meeting. If there are any remaining questions from the meeting participants, they can be asked here. This stage of the meeting is very straightforward and simple, but people leave the meeting feeling better and usually in agreement concerning the effectiveness and the importance of the meeting if there is a checkout phase. It allows the individuals closure and clarity, better preparing them to act on the solutions and actions just discussed.

Virtual problem solving meetings follow the same structure as face-to-face problem solving meetings. In both settings, Susanna would use root cause analysis and group memory as the tools to solve the problem at hand. Naturally, the meeting environment is different; instead of using a pen and flipchart to take notes and conduct the root cause analysis exercise, Susanna would use a keyboard and a virtual whiteboard. The different meeting environment goes beyond using a keyboard or a pen; it actually creates different group dynamics in which people interact differently.

It can be easy to think that problem solving is easier to do in face-to-face situations; tensions can be high, and to overcome a conflict or disagreement, people need to understand each other and make nice, right? Wouldn't this be easier in a face-to-face setting, where it is easier to read another person's emotions and understand them? Actually, this is not the case. A virtual environment has some big advantages for problem solving meetings. Virtual meetings are less personal, but this helps the problem solving process. If the meeting leader is correctly using group memory by writing down all the key points of the conversation and displaying them in a shared space for everyone to see, then the group memory will be the focal point of the meeting, not the emotional dynamic between two people. Honest feedback can be easier to give virtually too, since people will not be as worried about how someone will react to what they say.

ROOT CAUSE ANALYSIS

The morning after the problem solving meeting Susanna is at her desk, sifting through her emails and sipping on her morning latte when Bert 'accidentally' walks by.

"Good morning Susanna. That thing you did yesterday in the meeting where we listed the problems we had and then decided on the causes, that was damn smart."

"Thanks Bert!" said a happy Susanna.

Bert kept standing there, looking at Susanna, until he sheepishly asked, "Well, what was it?"

"They call it root cause analysis. It helps you define the actual problem when the issue seems a bit muddy. The basic principle is to explore cause and effect relationships using analysis that goes five levels deep. After doing that much analysis, you will typically find the root cause, along with the limits of the human brain for handling so many analytical levels," joked Susanna.

"Very clever. I wish our Management Team would try that too."

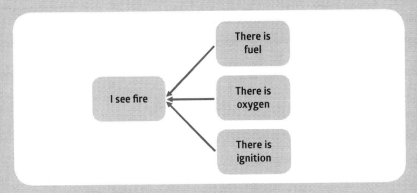

A cause and effect relationship.

The attraction of root cause analysis is that it enables you to look past the symptoms and the undesired effects of a problem to find the true cause of the problem. Practicing root cause analysis takes us deeper into analysis and avoids the common mistake of focusing on the wrong problems[*]. The tool for root cause analysis used by Susanna, called a current reality tree, works well in team settings and functions as a team-building tool. The real cause of a problem is identified, and then solutions are generated together by the group. In the problem solving meeting facilitated by Susanna, we see that they started with the undesired effect, which was poor sales. It took them five levels of analysis before they reached the root cause, which was the arrogant attitude of management. Usually the root cause is identified with five levels of analysis, and the root cause is typically an attitude or belief.

There is little difference in using root cause analysis virtually or in face-to-face settings. Virtually, you screen share a virtual whiteboard where participants can add their input remotely. In face-to-face meetings, post-it notes and a large sheet of paper taped to the wall would be the tools of choice for creating a current reality tree for the root cause analysis exercise. Either way, the steps are the same. One important detail of root cause analysis is that it only is effective with small

---

[*]   Root Cause Analysis is a broad field, with many different tools and techniques that can be used. In this book Susanna focuses on one method called *the current reality tree*. This method, introduced by the communications theorist Eliyahu Goldratt, has been a cornerstone in the field of root cause analysis.

groups. The logic systems of each individual are very complex, and the analysis, sharing, and discussion of many different logic systems, is simply too big a task and too time consuming to be practical in large groups. It is best to use root cause analysis in small meetings with less than six participants, with three participants being optimal.

The six steps of root cause analysis

1. Start with the undesired effects and build the cause-and-effect chain downwards

2. Add factors that contribute to, and cause the undesired effects

3. Check the logic of connections and draw arrows from the cause to the effect

4. Locate root causes (entities with outbound arrow only). If a root cause is responsible for over 70 % of symptoms, that is the core problem.

5. Draw your sphere of influence

6. Select one or more problems within your sphere of influence

Susanna felt good about the positive feedback. When you facilitate, people do not always acknowledge the value of the person designing and running the process. They are just happy with the content of the meeting and the results. Susanna had used a typical problem solving process; problem, solution, and actions. This time she was particularly happy that she used root cause analysis for clarifying the problem. Susanna had noticed that organizations often try to solve problems without first thinking about what the problem really is. Root cause analysis is an invaluable tool when you want to clarify existing complex problems. It is less effective when you want to create something totally new.

The conflict regarding the number of customer visits that Sales Team members had to do was a typical system-level problem. Sales were decreasing, and the most obvious solution was to activate sales. If the system does not work, the people typically just blame each other and run, run, and finally run some more until they get too tired and burn out, or the business dies. It is only through deeper understanding of the system that we can create better organizations.

BENEFITS, CHALLENGES, AND APPLICATION OF ROOT CAUSE ANALYSIS

Benefits
- Problems tend to come in different levels. Helps people see the true nature of problems.
- A true eye opener. People tend to see problems on the surface level, and the true problem is may be a surprise.

Challenges
- All people have different logic and it is very difficult to reach agreement, especially in a larger group. If you get stuck with a group, it may be easier to get an agreement on the problem itself than forcing everyone to agree on causal relations.

Application
- Helps arguing people to agree on the problem and to see the real issues. Typically, people argue about solutions and they can not reach agreement before they agree on a problem.
- Effective in clarifying complex problems.

I am getting good at this, realized Susanna. She thought that she would give George a call to brag a bit about her success to him. Susanna filled George in about how she used facilitation tools and root cause analysis to resolve Bert and Matthew's conflict. She felt good, and she deserved to celebrate. Right now, any work-related stress seemed

10,000 miles away. Unfortunately for Susanna, there are ups and downs in life and at work. Despite her feeling on top of the world right now, she was soon going to experience the other side of the coin.

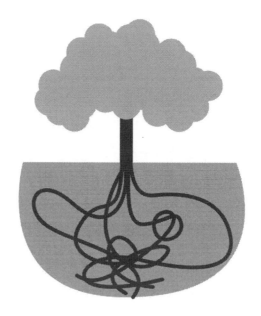

CHAPTER 6:

DEVELOPING A STAKEHOLDER COMMUNICATION PLAN

It is 10:44 at night, and Susanna is awake. She is sitting at her desk, unable to sleep or relax. Things were going smoothly and the Team was adjusting to recent changes, but Susanna felt her stress levels rising bit by bit each day.

I hate this, she thinks. Somehow, that thought does not capture the severity of her mood, so she tries again.

This is horrible! Every time someone wants something they call me and ask me how to handle things…even though the question usually has nothing to do with me. Can't people see I have enough going on without having to police every interaction or give advice on how to do every little thing?!?! This is killing me right now and I need something to change.

Susanna knows that something must be done, so she opens her laptop, and begins to type.

Dear Dream Team,

I am inviting you all to an optional virtual meeting next Friday. The objective of this meeting is to create a stakeholder communication plan. Who do we need to spend a lot of time communicating with? How should we interact with these people? Who can we spend less time dealing with? Who should be talking to these people? Keeping all of this in mind, click the link below to join the meeting, which will be at 10:00 in the morning (BST).

Enthusiastically Yours,
Susanna

Early Friday morning Susanna opened her computer. Ten participants had accepted the invitation and five declined. Matthew even sent an email apologizing, saying that although the meeting seemed very interesting, he was unable to attend due to finally finding and scheduling a meeting with a potentially important customer. Susanna appreciated Matthew's message. She was disappointed that Matthew was unable to attend but she understood why he couldn't make it.

Ten o'clock came around and the meeting began. Susanna was in her office, waiting for everyone to get logged into the virtual meeting software. As Susanna waited for the stragglers to arrive and get situated, she posted the following in group chat;

What are your expectations for today's meeting? What issues and problems do you hope will be clearer after today? Feel free to comment in the group chat.

During the check-in phase it became obvious everyone was enthusiastic about the meeting. Rita's comment summed up the general mood:

Our work seems so chaotic and I just want to understand who we should be focusing our attention on and why.

After greeting the participants and presenting the outline of the meeting, Susanna begins. "Our success as a team is not only in our hands. We are also dependent on others for our success. We need external help from outside the team and sometimes from outside the company. These people that can help us are called stakeholders. Please list as many of our stakeholders that you can think of in the chat. You have three minutes." Then Susanna highlighted the group chat screen and shared it with everyone in the meeting. She waited a moment, her eyes focused on the screen. Slowly but surely names begin to appear in the chat one by one, and after five minutes over two dozen names are listed in the shared group chat.

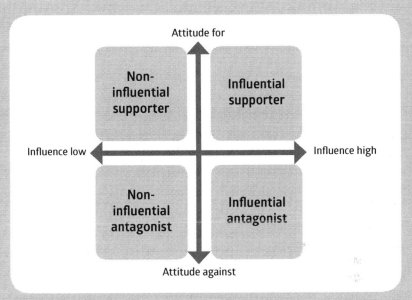

A slide where stakeholders can be categorized based on opinion and influence.

Once her team produced the list of stakeholders, Susanna pulls up a new slide on her screen which she shares with everyone.

"On this slide you can see two axes. The first axis shows the influence a stakeholder has; low influence on the left and running towards high influence on the right. The vertical axis is the attitudes axis. This summarizes what they think about us. Do they like us? Hate us? Are they indifferent? Their feelings and views determine where we place them on this axis. The attitudes change from poor to good as we move from the bottom to the top of the axis. I want you to place the stakeholders you listed in chat somewhere on the grid. If you do not agree on the placement of a name, you can move it to a place where you think it fits better. This is an individual activity for now. Discussion time will come later so please remember, no talking."

Susanna watched as the names began to appear on the grid. She could tell that there was some disagreement on the placement of names, as there was plenty of movement on the screen. But after a while, the names found their homes and stopped jumping around the screen.

During her time as a manager, Susanna learned that allowing a moment of time for silent reflection before discussion allowed people to gather their thoughts and to think critically about the topic at hand. If a discussion was opened immediately some people would jump right in and begin speaking. Others would continue to think about the problem and remain quiet, or even worse, tune out and have their minds wander.

After a while, no new names were appearing on the grid, so Susanna knew that it was time to continue.

"Susanna here. I see the names have all found their right places. You can see that the slide where you placed the stakeholder names was divided into four sections. These four sections of the slide represent the four types of stakeholders.

The first type of stakeholder is a non-influential antagonist. This is the Accounting and Finance manager Mr. Owlhill that hates our team for some reason. Thank goodness he does not have much influence over budgets. He is an antagonist, but he is not influential. As long as his influence remains low we do not need to put too much effort into making him happy.

The second type of stakeholder is like our marketing manager Mr. Watson. Like Mr. Owlhill, he too is not supportive of a lot of our team projects and initiatives, but unfortunately, he has direct control over our marketing budget and can influence our success or failure in a big way. He is powerful, and he is not aligned with our goals which makes him an influential antagonist. We should really find out what is bothering that guy and coordinate our work better with his. He is an example of a person we need to spend a lot of time and team resources on to win over.

We also seem to have lots of non-influential supporters and I see they could be used to support our cause. These are the third type of stakeholder. They are great to have, but unfortunately, they cannot do much in determining the success or failure of our team.

Finally, our key customer Mrs. Goldiamond is an influential supporter. She is ready and willing to tell the whole world that we have the greatest fruits on earth! In addition to her great attitudes about our company, she has the money to make purchases that significantly affect our bottom line. We need to think about how we can keep her happy so that we continue to have her support.

Now I am going to split you in three groups. Each group will be assigned eight stakeholders to think about. In these groups I want you to think of concrete ideas about how to communicate with each stakeholder, depending on whether they are an influential or non-influential supporter, or influential or non-influential antagonist. Please remember to write your ideas on the whiteboard. Are you ready? You have thirty minutes to come up with solutions."

The team members began to intensely discuss the stakeholders and after half an hour re-joined as one large group. They seemed to have done a good job with the exercise, producing excellent ideas.

"Susanna here again. Great job identifying the stakeholders and brainstorming effective ways to communicate with them. Now it is time to assign roles and decide who deals with which stakeholders. But first let's clarify the rules. You can take responsibility for any stakeholder by just writing your name right next to the name of a stakeholder, but as your boss I am responsible for aligning activities and I want to have the last word."

"Explain something to me please," Tony Dingle said. "What do you mean by, 'who deals with the stakeholder?' Let's say that there is someone who is important to talk to, and someone else signs up to communicate with them. Am I supposed to ignore them? Can I still make small talk with them? I don't really see the point of assigning a contact person from our team to a specific person. All of us already talk to everyone anyways."

"Thanks for the question and feedback Tony. The idea behind stakeholder analysis is so that all of us know how to prioritise our interactions with important people outside of our team. Remember last year when we were trying to get an increase in our travel budget?"

The team did in fact remember; it was a debacle and a bit of an embarrassment for them, even a year later. The team, desperate for an increase in their allowed budget, had pestered Bert about it non-stop. Bert ended up yelling at Susanna to 'call off her dogs', as he hardly could even make it down the hallway to his own office without several different Sales Team members pestering him with questions or requests about the new budget. The situation ended with the Sales Team getting an increase in their budget, and also Bert screaming at Susanna about how 'bloody annoying' the whole situation was.

Susanna explained to her Sales Team, "We assign the stakeholders to a specific team member in order to avoid what happened last year with Bert. All of you can obviously interact normally with someone else's assigned person, but it is not your job to seek out conversation with them about our projects or try to win them over."

The meeting continued, and the division of labour and responsibility went well. Team members were not hesitant to take responsibility. Rose Middleton wrote her name next to the big customer, Mrs. Goldia-mond. Tony Dingle decided to take on the challenge of dealing with Marketing manager Mr. Watson. Susanna was satisfied. Everything wasn't perfect though, as one stakeholder seemed unwanted by all.

This lonely stakeholder was Bert. Bert was supportive of the Sales Team, and proud of their work. He also was extremely high up in the company and very powerful, which made him exceptionally intimidating to deal with.

"Doesn't anyone want to deal with Bertram?" asked Susanna, as the silence in the room stretched on for what seemed like half an hour.

Finally, Rita Barmyfield opened her mouth. "Rita here. I'm sorry Susanna. I know Bert is a real pain in the butt with all of his enthusiasm about new and unrealistic ideas on how to run the business. And I know you would like someone else to deal with him but hey, you are the boss here and you have to deal with your own superiors."

Damn. It's difficult to hear the truth thought Susanna as she reluctantly wrote her own name next to Bert's.

After writing down her name next to Bert's, all the stakeholders were accounted for and each had a name of a team member written beside it.

"Thanks for your hard work today," said Susanna to her team. "After this meeting, I hope that all of you have a better idea of how to prioritise your communication with people outside of the team. I am also happy to see that you all have assigned stakeholders to yourselves. I hope that this will streamline communication between our team and the rest of the company. I will make a slide with all of our stakeholders on it and who signed up to communicate with them, and I will share this with the entire team via email in the next day or two. Are there any questions?"

"I have one," said Rose. "Let's say that in a week or two, I talk with someone else on the team and we decide that we want to switch stakeholders for some reason. How do we do this? I guess we should OK it with you first...?"

Susanna, upon hearing Roses question, had a quick flashback and imagined people constantly coming up to her, asking about switching stakeholders. *It would be as if we never had this meeting at all! Instead of asking me all the time how to talk to someone, people would be asking me IF they could talk to someone. I better stop this idea before it starts.*

"Great question Rose, thanks. I do not need any of you to OK it with me if you want to change stakeholders. I am going to create a shared document and any of you can edit it if you want to change something. The idea behind this meeting is to empower all of you and remove me a bit from the stakeholder communication process."

The group did not have any other questions, so Susanna asked for feedback by having the group rate the meeting; one for a horrible meeting, five for a wonderful meeting, and something in between for, well, something in between. As the group was answering the poll, Susanna saw mostly four's and five's. She was happy, and it looked like the group was too.

ANALYSIS

This chapter opened with Susanna being stressed. Susanna was at the centre of all communication between her team, and that made her extremely busy. There was a lack of agreement about how her team should communicate with people outside of the team. Who should be responsible for communicating with customers, suppliers, or anyone else that team members would encounter in their work? Because her team had not identified or agreed on how to deal with stakeholders, the communication became the responsibility of the team leader. Instead of a unified plan of attack, everyone turned to Susanna for direction, leaving her overwhelmed and in a disagreeable mood.

Susanna used a stakeholder analysis to create a communication plan for her team. Every team has a goal, and stakeholders are on-board and enthusiastic, or they are resistant to it. The function of a communication plan is to identify and classify people into different groups so that resources, time and energy can be spent effectively in dealing with the different groups.

The people placed into the first category are the non-influential supporters. These people are your cheerleaders and form your fan club. Imagine a bakery opens and to generate business, free pastries are given away every Friday at noon. The non-influential supporters are the people that show up every Friday exactly at noon to eat the free pastries. They may be very friendly and rave to you about how good they taste, but they rarely make a purchase. They just take up chairs in your bakery, munching on the free pastries and drinking the complimentary tea. Non-influential supporters should be involved more in daily work. They are on your side and support you, and although they do not carry a lot of weight or influence, they can be made useful by doing tasks and contributing to the work load, which frees up other team resources.

If there are multiple individuals that are non-influential supporters, put them into a group. One company that specialized in business communication offered a free demo of their services in the form of a brief training course. The same people showed up week in and week out to participate in the demo, and to discuss the principles taught. They were enthusiastic and eager, but they were draining the company's resources. So, the company decided to start a free business communications network, and placed these people in it, which gave them a forum for discussion, and also resolved the problem of people abusing the free demo by attending each week.

The second category is known as the influential supporters. Influential supporters are best used as your lobbyists. These are people with influence who love what you do, so use them to shout your praises in meaningful ways. You can use them to provide testimonials. You can even have them interact with potential investors or other important contacts. Involving these people in the design process or procedural matters gives them a sense of investment in your company and ensures that they remain your supporters for a long time to come. So, give them a sense of involvement when it comes to the business, be it significant involvement or not. Examples of influential supporters can be investors, members of advisory boards, and hopefully members of management.

The third category is comprised of the influential antagonists. These people are your critics that have sway and power. Influential antagonists deserve an opportunity to express their concerns. Find out what their specific concerns are and explicitly address these. Make them feel comfortable that their views are not just being heard but also being acted upon and resolved when possible. This gives them a sense of ownership when it comes to decision making. Listening to their concerns and taking these concerns into account when making future business decisions can be therapeutic to the influential antagonists and keep big conflicts from occurring.

The fourth and final category is the non-influential antagonists. These are people with little influence or power who are critical of what you do. Non-influential antagonists do not deserve a whole lot of time or effort. Just be sure to remain polite to them and do not give them any additional reasons to dislike you.

These four groups are generally static, meaning that there is not a lot of movement or reclassifying of people from one group to another. If someone is classified as influential or non-influential, this typically stays true and does not change, although organizational restructuring within a company can lead to a person or group moving from one category to another.

In a perfect world all four groups would receive adequate attention and care regarding their issues and concerns. But in practice you need to pick your battles. What is the return on the energy that is spent in dealing with each of these groups? The point of a communication plan is to track where the energy goes and to ensure a good return on the time and energy of employees.

In the communication plan workshop, Susanna used a structure that was familiar to her; clarifying, solutions, and actions. This is the same structure she used in her face-to-face problem solving meeting.

Here, she opened the communication plan meeting by first explaining what a stakeholder is. She told her team that there were people outside of the team that either help or hurt the team's chances of success. She explained that these people were called stakeholders. Then Susanna instructed the group to list in a shared virtual chatroom all the stakeholders they could think of. Next, she pulled up a chart which had a specific quadrant for all four types of stakeholders. People then had to classify each stakeholder into what they felt was the correct area. After this was completed, Susanna let the group ask her any questions about the classification process. This was the last part of the clarifying stage.

When all of the stakeholders were properly classified, Susanna explained to the group how to communicate with each type of stakeholder. She let everyone know who was important to talk to and who wasn't. Susanna then put people into small groups and asked them to think of concrete ways to communicate with them. At this stage people already knew who they needed to talk to, and they were finding solutions and ideas about how best to do it. This was the solutions stage of the meeting.

Then, still in small groups, they began picking stakeholders they would contact. This was the actions stage of the meeting; people were planning specifically how they would communicate with important stakeholders, and the important questions of *who, what,* and *when* were answered during this stage.

The tool-specific structure of Susanna's stakeholder analysis meeting

Pre-Meeting
- Invitation with meeting info and brief explanation of the purpose of meeting.

Check-in
- Susanna presents the meeting agenda to the group and asks about expectations for the day in chat.

Clarifying
- Susanna defines stakeholder to the group and asks everyone to list different stakeholders in the group chat.
- Susanna asks the team to classify all stakeholders on a shared slide as either influential/non-influential, supporter/antagonist.

Solutions
- Susanna places people into small groups, and assigns each group a set of stakeholders. The groups then discuss how to best communicate with the stakeholders.

Action
- Susanna asks people to think about which stakeholders they should communicate with. People then sign their name next to a stakeholder to take responsibility for that person.

Check-out
- Susanna asks the group to rate the meeting on a scale of one to five with the virtual polling feature.

Check-in

↓

Clarifying
Solutions
Action

↓

Check-out

In just one workshop Susanna actually managed to delegate a big workload to her Team. She believed her life was going to become a lot easier now. However, delegating did not mean she was going to let go of all responsibility. These stakeholders were an important part of the success of the Sales Team, and as the manager Susanna was going to have to follow up on the outlined stakeholder communication plan in future meetings.

Looking back on the meeting, Susanna realized that she would have led it similarly if it was virtual or face-to-face. The stakeholder analysis would have been the same; in both cases the group is asked to think of a list of different stakeholders, and then classify them according to what type they are.

Susanna would then use small group discussion to have the group think of solutions and finally, people would commit to future actions.

The difference would be in the meeting environment. In the virtual meeting, Susanna had the group write stakeholder names onto a slide labelled with an axis separating the four kinds of stakeholders. If the meeting was face-to-face, meeting participants would need to write down stakeholder names onto post-it notes and then stand up, walk to the front of the room, and place them onto a graph that Susanna drew on a flipchart.

Is there anything that Susanna can't do? If her recent successes are any indication, then the answer must be no. With the help of virtual facilitation skills, she has proven to be up for any challenge.

Susanna was still a bit troubled though. While she truly believed that she was working with a wonderful team, she wanted something more. Recently she had noticed an increase in uneven information distribution throughout the team. Some people seemed to have their own methods of working, unique to themselves, that could really help others. *If only they could share all their talents with each other* thought Susanna one evening after work. And it was this specific thought that led Susanna on to her next leadership opportunity.

BENEFITS, CHALLENGES, AND APPLICATION OF STAKEHOLDER COMMUNICATION PLAN

Benefits
· Creates focus on most important stakeholders and saves resources
· Helps delegate responsibility

Challenges
· When you delegate responsibility you also lose control

Application
· Key tool for delegating responsibility for team members

CHAPTER 7:

TEAM DEVELOPMENT: INCREASING COLLABORATION

Susanna felt good about how things were progressing. The team was enthusiastic and committed to their goals. But Susanna was not satisfied. She felt that something could be done even better. Some team members had come to Susanna with problems that made it seem like the Team was not as connected as it should be.

In a recent discussion Matthew told Susanna that, "I have plenty of good customers that actually have offices all around Europe. I could easily turn one sale into something much larger, but that would mean I would be making sales in areas that are outside of my district and encroaching on the sales of my colleagues."

Susanna frowned slightly and thought for a moment. She then asked, "Why don't you just share this information about all those opportunities with the rest of the team? They could use your work as a reference."

"Suzy come on. I am busy enough as it is trying to get my own sales. I do not have time to line up a new potential opportunity and hand it over to someone else when I can focus on getting my own numbers up."

In another discussion Rita said, "I have invented a great process on how to record my orders. It saves me over fifteen minutes every day."

Susanna was very happy to hear this, as she was always looking for ways to save time and streamline the orders process. Susanna excitedly asked Rita when and how she planned on sharing this information with the rest of the team.

"I guess I could share this process with the team, but it would take me a couple of days to go through it with everyone and they still might decide not to implement my way of working just because they are scared of a new process."

Susanna was discouraged, but the comments by Matthew and Rita opened her eyes to the fact that something needed to be done. The team was performing well, but it still was not working as a unified unit. Susanna decided to put an end to this immediately.

She decided to act immediately and began typing another friendly email to her team members, which served as her trademark invitation to a virtual meeting.

Dear Dream Team,

You all continue to exceed expectations and have been doing a great job recently. But now is the time to become better than ever through improving our communication.

It is time to get to know each other's trade secrets and to share your own. Please prepare for the meeting by writing down ideas and working methods you can contribute to the team. Also, please list a few things that you would like to learn from the team. You can join the virtual meeting by clicking the link below. The meeting will take place Thursday afternoon at 16:00, London time. I'm looking forward to chatting with you all soon!

Your Very Own Virtual Manager,
Susanna

When Thursday afternoon rolled around, Susanna checked the responses to her invitation and she was pleasantly surprised that this time the whole team was able to attend. Susanna started the meeting by restating the day's goal; share the best individual working practices and information about clients. Next Susanna asked for the participants to write down their expectations in the chat. In twenty seconds she was able to see all the expectations of the group. Most of the participants had understood the concept of the meeting correctly and wrote things like, "Learn time saving ordering techniques", and "Find out ways to reduce the amount of weekly paperwork." Margaret had a slightly different idea about what the meeting would address, writing, "I want a raise."

Susanna was taken off guard and asked, "Margaret, could you elaborate a little please?"

"Sure thing Suze! Right now, sales are going really well, and since the meeting was about offers and needs, I need to take a vacation to Mallorca. I thought of asking for a raise and I expect you to offer me one."

Smiling, Susanna took this in stride and replied, "I'm sorry Margaret, but today you are going to have to talk about offers and needs with your team members and the discussion about your raise will have to wait until our quarterly one-on-one meeting."

Margaret understood, but seemed slightly discouraged that she would have to wait at least another month before she could continue to vacation plan.

With the group online and engaged, Susanna began the needs and offers activity which would be the vehicle to achieve the meeting goal of sharing working practices and uniting the team. Susanna opened the virtual whiteboard, displaying the names and telephone numbers of the entire team.

"I have written down the phone numbers and names of the entire team. You will notice that each person on the list is either an odd or an even number. The odd numbers will call the even numbers. Matt, you are the first one on the list. That means that you will call Margaret who is second on the list, OK?"

Matt and the others seem to understand. Susanna then gave her final instructions for this activity. "You have fifteen minutes to discuss your offers and needs. After the fifteen minutes are up, we all will come back to this meeting and record your agreements on the whiteboard. If you have any problems I am staying online and can help."

The work proceeded nicely, and in fifteen minutes the participants came back to the virtual meeting and started writing their key takeaways and action points on the shared virtual whiteboard. Most of the actions were related to customers, but some of the information was not quite what Susanna had expected. Margaret wrote down, "Matt just taught me that when asking for a salary raise from Suzy, I should ask for just a small raise now and then a bigger one in half a year. That strategy seems to work the best for him."

Oh no! These guys are getting to know me too well, thought Susanna, and the meeting continued. "We have three rounds of offers and needs negotiations. During the next round the even numbers call the odd numbers below. Except the last number on the list calls the first one, meaning Rosy calls Matt."

Suzy decided to do the third round a little differently. "During the third round anyone can call anybody else that they want. If the number is busy, too bad. You were too slow, and you need to choose a different number.

Everyone got to work on the activity and once again were productive. Many conversations were taking place as people called each other, eager to share their tips and learn new ones. The virtual whiteboard was filling up with agreements about how team members could help one another. Susanna was hopeful that the energy and collaboration that was visible in this activity would carry on going forward.

During the check-out stage, Susanna wanted individual comments from each team member.

"I was talking to people I had never talked before. That was interesting."

"I never knew that we had so many common customers. Suzy, this stuff was beneficial."

"This was good for the team spirit."

"I was able to talk to only three colleagues, I want to talk to everybody."

"At first this sounded stupid and I thought I had nothing to offer, but when others started talking I realised what I can offer and what I really need from the team."

ANALYSIS

Susanna was elated after the session. The amount of cooperation she had been able to create in one session was remarkable, and she did so with a simple process. All she used was a simple 'needs and offers' activity, which is an effective tool used by facilitators. First, she had the participants call each other and discuss their offers and needs. This means that they share what they could contribute to the group (offers) and what they hoped to gain from the others (needs).

Susanna's virtual Team development meeting, which was based around needs and offers negotiations

Pre-Meeting
- Susanna sends invitations to her team giving them an idea of what to expect in the meeting and also a pre-meeting assignment to help them prepare.

Check-in
- Going through the meeting schedule and objectives.
- Susanna asks everyone to list their expectations for the meeting in the chat.

Needs and offers negotiations
- Susanna displays a slide with the name and phone number of all meeting attendees.
- She labels everyone as either 'A' or 'B' and instructs participants to call the other.
- People talk in pairs about what kinds of support they want from each other and also what kind of help they can offer. People write down on shared virtual whiteboard concrete action points; what, who, when
- Pair discussion is repeated twice more in different groups.

Check-out
- Susanna asks for everyone to speak briefly about how they felt the meeting went. There is also one last opportunity for questions or additional comments.

Check-in

↓

Needs and offers activity

↓

Check-out

Next, they listed what they learned and what new actionable behaviours can be adopted based on the new information they learned. Besides getting team members to share information with each other, this activity revisits and solves the problem we saw Susanna struggle with earlier in this book; being the sole information holder and the one responsible for providing answers to everyone's problems and questions. The needs and offers negotiation activity allowed for the group to establish what each member could contribute and what problems and issues each member could assist with. This is an activity which naturally delegates tasks and greatly improves the flow of information and dramatically increases cooperation within a team. It works well in both virtual and face-to-face environments.

Susanna's needs and offers activity

Check-in
· Going through the program and objectives.
· Susanna asks everyone to post their expectations for the meeting.

Needs and offers negotiations
· Susanna asks participants to individually list ideas about what they could offer the team and what kind of support they need from the team.
· Posting and reading the offers and needs in silence
· Opening the marketplace. Susanna invites the participants to talk to as many people as possible and to post action points (which you may call deals) in a concrete form; what, who, when.
· Ground rules:
    – Try to balance giving and taking. Each deal does not have to be mutual
    – Talk to one person at a time, it tends to be more efficient
· Evaluating results with all participants. There is also one last opportunity for questions or additional comments.

Check-out
· Susanna asks for everyone to speak briefly about how they felt the meeting went.

In a face-to-face environment you just have the participants share their needs and offers in pairs or small groups. Once sharing is complete, you have the participants record their concrete action points on a flipchart that is visible to all.

In face-to-face workshops participants can see when others are free to connect, and Susanna may let the people self-organise the exchange of ideas. Susanna simply creates a marketplace for exchanging needs and offers by asking the participants to list their needs and offers on a large piece of paper and to post the papers on the wall. Then she asks people to read through the offers and needs in order to find potential partners. If someone agrees to help fulfil the needs of someone else, this is called a deal. Finally, she opens the marketplace by inviting the participants to connect with as many people as they can within half an hour and to record their action points on the flipchart in a concrete form that includes the what, who, when. While carrying out the offers and needs negotiations, it is important to remind the participants that every exchange or deal does not have to be two sided, in a balanced exchange you both give and get, but when working in a team each individual exchange does not have to be balanced. Also, she reminds the participants that they should be talking to one person at a time which tends to be more effective than forming larger groups. In the end Susanna asks participants to read and evaluate the results.

BENEFITS, CHALLENGES AND APPLICATION OF NEEDS AND OFFERS NEGOTIATIONS

Benefits
· Creates new connections within team
· Increases team co-operation
· Energising and motivating activity

Challenges
· This activity may produce too many actions points

Application
· Key activity to increase team co-operation

THE TRUST FORMULA

During her long career as a manager, Susanna has learned that teams naturally form small cliques. People tend to collaborate only with their favourite people. She believes that a key task as a leader is to break up these cliques and help team members co-operate with each other. This is no easy task, but Susanna is an experienced leader and she has a solution for this.

Susanna believed that communication within the Team would improve if she created more trust and connections between her team members. If team members do not naturally interact with one another, the manager has to create the time, place, and purpose for connecting with each other. This can be done either virtually or face-to-face. The secret behind team trust is self-disclosure; sharing something about yourself. Disclosing personal information creates bonds and humanizes other team members, all of which leads to better communication and team work.

The difference between the connections of a typical team and the connections of a dream team.

In this exercise Susanna used offers and needs as a purpose for connecting team members and it proved to be both a practical and successful approach. Sales Team members found sources of help from people that they normally did not rely on, and just as importantly, they realized how they could help others.

During her facilitation training, her mentor George was very fond of quoting the formula for creating team trust:

TEAM TRUST = CONNECTIONS x SELF-DISCLOSURE

Trust increases as people have the chance to connect with others and share about themselves while learning about the other person.

All of these ideas were recorded on the virtual whiteboard during the meeting, and Susanna, knowing the importance of group memory, made sure to send them to everyone after the meeting ended.

In this session, Susanna used the prompt of offers and needs to begin conversations between team members. Yet Susanna could have used about any non-work-related theme to get the team talking with each other. A person's hobbies, hometown, or favourite things (food, places etc.) all would have worked fine. Work-related topics such as sharing best practises, work roles and team roles also would have served the purpose of this activity. It's true that talking about spaghetti or pet cats is much more trivial than the discussions during the needs and offers activity, but that is OK. In developing a team dynamic, sometimes the only step the team leader needs to take is to make the rest of the team chat with one another. Susanna decided to help walk them through the specific ways that they could help one another, but if she didn't do this and instead had them talk about something trivial, the team members would have still broken silos (systems or processes that operate in isolation) and created more trust.

CHAPTER 8:

TEAM DEVELOPMENT: AGREEING ON GROUND RULES

In the weeks following the workshop, Susanna noticed the Sales Team relying on each other more. Questions that normally would have been emailed to Susanna were now being asked and answered within the team. *I could get used to this*, Susanna thought happily. But in the back of her mind she knew that there was room for improvement, and soon enough the next opportunity presented itself.

It was early in the morning and Susanna had just arrived at work. Susanna scarcely had the chance to sit down and begin attacking her unread emails when a phone icon flashed on her screen. Next to the red flashing phone icon, which signified a request for a video-call, was a picture of Margaret. Susanna accepted the call, and Margaret's face filled the screen.

"Good Morning Margaret! What a nice surprise it is seeing you this morning."

Skipping pleasantries, Margaret jumped right in to what was on her mind.

"The rest of the team is not sharing info with me. I thought that things would improve after our most recent session where we shared what skills we can provide to the rest of the team, but now it is even worse!"

Susanna wondered how things could possibly take a turn for the worse after such a positive meeting, but Margaret was not going to keep her in suspense for long.

"Before, no one in the Sales Team communicated well with me, but they did not really communicate well with each other, either! At least I felt like an equal of sorts. Now the entire team is closer than ever! I know this is true because I can see their schedules update in real-time with conference calls and collaborative sessions. They make decisions together on their sales areas but do not tell me anything. And they don't even bother recording their meetings or taking notes. Imagine me Susanna, booking meeting spaces for them and confirming virtual meeting times for everyone, but never an invitation for me, I am just the secretary after all..."

Margaret ended the call a few minutes later. Susanna managed to make her feel a bit better, reminding her that she was hardly *just* a secretary, but rather a valuable part of the Sales Team.

How can I help the Sales Team realize Margaret's full skill-set? What can be done so that she feels a bit more included in everything?

Susanna did not have an immediate answer to these questions. She kept thinking that she needed to conduct a workshop where the talents and abilities of each team member were outlined, and then matched with the needs of the team...but she just did that in the most recent workshop!

Later that same week, Susanna found herself chatting with Alfonso, who was uncharacteristically frustrated. He was known among the team as being ever-the-optimist and hearing him complain was quite the shock to Susanna.

"I have sent all team members a personal email inviting them to give me sales statistics that I promised to send you and Bert. Everyone knows it is my job to compile these figures twice a month, but two weeks have passed, and I have only received three replies. And what do these replies say?! 'We will do it later, Alfonso'. Yesterday I sent everyone a reminder, and I have received nothing. No-one bothered to even tell me if they are planning to send me their sales numbers. We need rules for the team to follow... a code of conduct that spells out how to appropriately interact with others, because some people could benefit from such information. And the first rule? If you get an email from Alfonso, you reply immediately!"

Susanna managed to calm Alfonso down a bit by assuring him that she would come up with something.

Rules rules rules....I hate having to introduce even more rules thought Susanna. She thought back to her time in school where rules were constructed to get unruly kids to obey and follow instructions. Susanna had an idea in her head that effective leadership meant relinquishing control and trusting people. Introducing new rules to manage behaviour felt counterintuitive to this idea, but Margaret and Alfonso's comments got Susanna thinking, *perhaps we need a set of ground rules to help us work better together.*

The World Fruit Conference in Amsterdam was approaching, and Susanna knew that this event provided a great opportunity to talk with the entire team about any new rules. Fruit & Loading Inc.'s head boss Bert made it a priority to fly the entire team out to attend the conference. He believed that the event was not just important for networking and following industry trends, but also was a fantastic team building activity. Every year around the time of the Conference, Bert would send out an email to the entire company to make sure that everyone was ready and enthusiastic for the trip.

Knowing that her entire Sales Team would be there and in good spirits, she decided to use this occasion to conduct a workshop on creating ground rules. Susanna booked a conference room on the top floor of the Okura hotel, and after the second day of the conference she invited everyone there.

"I hope the conference is going well for all of you," Susanna began.

The mood was relaxed, and Susanna made sure to have some nice apple cider available. After all, they were attending a special conference, and she wanted her team to enjoy themselves a bit.

"I called you all here for this workshop so that we can work together and establish some common rules for our team. I hope that these rules will improve the way we communicate and work."

Around the room, cups of cider were slowly lowered, and team members exchanged surprise glances. Abigail, who had worked with Susanna for years, thought that this was a joke.

"Nice one Suze. Surely you have not called all of us together to this beautiful room complete with stunning views and nice cold cider just to talk about rules?"

A few people nodded in agreement, and Abigail went on, "One of the first things that come to mind when we think of you as a leader is how hands-off you are. You trust us Susanna. This is what allows us to do our jobs well. We know that you have faith in our abilities and are not setting up a million rules that we must follow."

"First off, Abigail, thank you for the compliment. And yes, you are 100 % correct that I trust the team and have the utmost confidence in each one of you. That is not the purpose of introducing more rules. The purpose of this workshop is to create rules which will help us work better with each other. I do not intend to waste everyone's time and go through rules which are not needed; we will not be discussing the right time to arrive to work, and how to use the company credit card properly. Instead the goal is to become more efficient and effective in how we interact with each other. This also applies to me. Enough talk, I think the best explanation is to begin so you can all see for yourselves what I mean."

After explaining the goals of the workshop and aligning expectations, Susanna introduced the first task. "Think about what working in this team is like. List the behaviours and working habits that frustrate you. You have two minutes to make your lists. Please begin."

The group hesitated for a moment, and Susanna understood why. It's rare to ask people to list what frustrates them about working with their team mates, especially for a company like Fruit & Loading Inc., emphasizes a positive and supportive company culture, but after a brief period of hesitation, people warmed to the task and began filling their papers.

Next Susanna asked everyone to pair up and share their lists together.

"After talking with your partner, I want each pair to agree on what the two worst behaviours are that you have on your lists. What I mean by worst, is most damaging to the team performance."

After about five minutes of discussion, Susanna could tell that the pairs were mostly ready, so she instructed them to write down their two worst behaviours on a piece of paper, and tape it up on the wall.

"Make sure you write large enough so the entire group can read your ideas," Susanna reminded the group.

Ideas describing unproductive team behaviours appeared on the wall. Most were very familiar behaviours that Susanna could relate to. The pairs presented the behaviours and Susanna said, "Great! Now we are going to get a collective group agreement of which are the most important behaviours by voting." As Susanna said this, she was walking around the room handing out small circular stickers.

"Each pair now has three small stickers. These are you votes. Your job as a pair is to place your stickers next to what you think are the most important things listed on the wall. You are free to use all of your votes on just one idea, or you can vote once for three different things-whatever you think is best."

When everyone was finished, Susanna counted the votes and presented the key behaviours to avoid;

- people are not mentally present in meetings
- no-one answers emails
- arguments in meetings
- lack of information of the decisions made by/concerning others
- unfair distribution of work

Susanna formed five groups and gave each group one of the key behaviours to work with.

"We have the behaviours we want to change. Now let's find solutions! As a group I want you to think of ideas about how your group's key behaviour can be changed. You have five minutes to do this, and please let me know if you have any questions."

Susanna also instructed each group to take notes and write down their ideas in clear, full sentences that others can understand even without presentations.

Five minutes later Susanna walked around the room and collected each group's paper. "We are going to remain in the same groups for now to continue discussing these behaviours. The key change is going to be that I am going to mix up the papers, so you will continue the discussion with a different key behaviour. Use the paper from the other group as a starting point for your discussion."

Susanna gave more time for discussion, occasionally stopping everyone for a moment to rotate papers and topics.

When each group had brainstormed solutions for each key behaviour, Susanna collected their papers and taped them to the wall.

Susanna stepped back and looked at the five large pieces of paper that were filled with the solutions. The team had managed to find at least five or six solutions for each key behaviour to avoid, ranging from simple solutions like, *actively listen to others during meetings,* to moderate policy changes like *answer all emails within 24 hours,* to huge initiatives *like automate processes to decrease shared repetitive tasks among team members.*

"Well, judging by the number of solutions that all of you were able to come up with, I can see that I should have given you more difficult problems! Maybe in our next workshop you all can end world hunger and cure cancer! Stand up and take a look at your work."

Everyone stood up and enjoyed their results. Matthew was especially impressed.

"You know Susanna, I never realized how easy your job is. It must be nice to be in charge of a team like us that has all of the answers."

Susanna chuckled along with the rest of her team at Matthews comment, as she thought to herself, *I like his enthusiasm, but I can already tell he will be a handful in negotiating a new salary during his performance review.*

Susanna continued on. "Now we are going to vote in our small groups. What solutions are most important for us to adopt in order to improve the way we work? Each group will get ten stickers this time. Just like the last round of voting, I want you to talk together and reach a consensus about where to place your stickers. If you think one idea is brilliant and the rest unimportant, put all ten by the one brilliant idea. Or, distribute them evenly; it is up to you and your group entirely. Go!"

The small groups spread around the room and begin chatting intensively. Susanna hears several debates about what the best solutions are; the activity is working just as she hoped. After a few moments, some of the groups have reached an agreement and begin placing their stickers next to solutions.

With all the stickers placed, Susanna asked everyone to return to their seats so everyone could see which solutions were selected. The solution with the most votes was *actively listen and participate in meetings*.

Although there were dozens and dozens of solutions written on the pieces of paper, Susanna noticed that 6 stood out from the rest in that they got many more votes. Susanna pointed this out to the group. "OK, we can see that six proposed solutions seem to be much more popular than the rest. Let's review these together to see how we feel about these being adopted as the ground rules for our team. We are going to vote with our thumbs. A thumb facing down means that you do not agree with these ground rules. Stick your thumb to the side if you partially agree with them and give thumbs up if you are happy with the ground rules. On the count of three we will vote; one, two, three!"

Most of the thumbs are up, but a few participants are just OK with the ground rules and one thumb is facing down. "Margaret, you do not like these ground rules?"

Margaret shook her head no. "I think that our solution of further automating the order receival process is just what we need to balance the unfair work distribution. I know that when it is my turn to process received orders, I feel overloaded with work and I do not have time to keep up with my daily tasks. But that solution is clearly not a ground rule."

Worried, Susanna asked, "What would you like us to do with this solution and ground rules?"

"I think that we should deal with the automation, but not include it in ground rules. All other ground rules are just fantastic," Margaret continues. Susanna promises to deal with the automation together with the IT-department. The ground rules have been accepted and Susanna promises to follow-them up in the next team meeting.

Finally, the workshop ends with a brief review and a chance for questions and comments.

"Before we leave to enjoy the rest of our cider and the rest of the night, I want to give one last chance for any questions or comments that may remain."

Alfonso raised his hand. He thought that it was important that the team agreed that arguments in meetings are a problem, and he was hopeful that simply by identifying this problem as a team, it may already be partially fixed.

Several participants were especially excited about the proposed solution for email replies, and Abigail summarized the discussion on this by saying, "It may have its problems, but our new idea off answering all emails within 24 hours is excellent. I hate being uncertain if someone is going to write me back and feeling like I am talking to myself."

After the group shared their final questions and comments, Susanna realized that it was nearly ten at night. She was ready to hurry off to bed, while the group splintered off to enjoy a beautiful Saturday night.

THE MOST FRUSTRATING BEHAVIOURS OF SUSANNA'S TEAM AND THEIR PRIORITISED SOLUTIONS

Lack of information of decisions concerning others
· invite everyone affected by decisions to the meetings

People are not mentally present in the meetings
· if you attend, listen and participate actively

Arguments in meetings
· we always seek consensus, if no consensus, Suzy decides

No-one answers emails
· do not send emails requiring action without prior agreement with the receiver
· answer all emails within 24 hours

Unfair distribution of work during peak sales time
· restructure and automatize the order receival process.

ANALYSIS

Ground rules set guidelines for team interaction. They can define how we communicate, work, and make decisions as a group. Their purpose is to remove distractions, so everyone works more efficiently.

AREAS THAT OFTEN NEED GROUND RULES

· How to work during peak or busy times

· How to distribute work

· Decision making

· Helping each other

· How to keep the work atmosphere positive

· Meeting practices

· Conflict resolution

· Team communication; how to keep the team informed

The best ground rules come out of retrospectives. When you focus on existing behaviours that hinder team productivity, you tend to get the most practical set of rules. That is why Susanna asked the team to list the most frustrating behaviours the team encountered in their work. This is not an easy topic, however. It is much more common for an employee to share positive feedback about their workmates, and it can be problematic for someone to come up with a list of frustrations or annoying behaviours about how others work.

Listening to someone else list things that annoy them about working with you or in your team can be even more difficult, and it sometimes causes arguments or people playing the *blame game*; pointing the finger at someone else and claiming, "it's not my fault!"

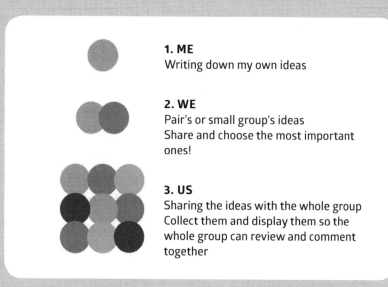

1. ME
Writing down my own ideas

2. WE
Pair's or small group's ideas
Share and choose the most important ones!

3. US
Sharing the ideas with the whole group
Collect them and display them so the whole group can review and comment together

The Me-We-Us method for encouraging and facilitating participation and discussion of team members.

Susanna used a tool called Me-We-Us to identify the most frustrating behaviours and to create a safe environment for the Sales Team to discuss sensitive topics. In the first stage called the Me-stage, participants think on their own. Giving time for individual reflection allows people to come up with more ideas. During the second stage, the We-stage, people discuss in pairs or small groups, and then are asked to choose the most frustrating behaviours. Sharing ideas in small groups gives a chance for ideas to be further developed. A group of three has enough people in it to relieve the pressure of speaking in front of a large group, and it is still small enough for a single person to have enough time to share their thoughts in detail. Finally, in the Us- stage, Susanna asked participants to write the ideas on a large piece of paper with big letters. These papers are then posted where the entire group can see, and the ideas are presented.

To reach group consensus and prioritise ideas, Susanna used the dot-voting method. This tool requires pairs or small groups to discuss the content and then prioritise it. This is a safe way for a group to share their opinions and find priorities, and Susanna likes to use it when dealing with difficult topics.

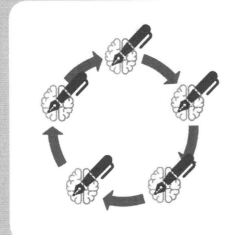

Small groups write their ideas on flipchart papers. Papers are then rotated between groups and people build on the ideas generated by other groups.

Group Brainwriting is an effective method for collecting solutions for multiple questions.

After finding the key behaviours that asked for ground rules, she formed small groups and gave each one a topic to discuss. She instructed each group to propose solutions to their topic and write their ideas on a large piece of flip-chart paper. After that, she rotated papers and let the new groups read and add ideas. Finally, she asked pairs to prioritise the best solutions with stickers. This way of working is called group brainwriting and it works particularly well when you have multiple questions to address. It is always more effective and more activating to have a group split up and have many discussions at a time, than to have one big group discussion. Often in large group discussions the more outgoing and louder people will dominate, and their ideas will overshadow those of a quieter person.

In the end, she asked the team to check if ground rules selected represent concrete behaviours that can be followed-up on. Sometimes the team members suggest ground rules that are vague and difficult to review. For instance, a rule like, *trust your team mates* is just not concrete enough.

To be effective, this ground rule needs to be developed further. For instance, *establish two-way communication by asking questions and giving frequent feedback* might work better as a ground rule that creates trust.

Asking a group to think of examples of a ground rule as it applies to their own work can help define it.

A good number of ground rules to come up with in a session range from three to six. Any more than this and they can be hard to remember and even harder to follow. That is why group prioritisation activities like dot-voting are key as they allow a group to define what is the most important for them.

Susanna told the team that she will have a follow-up meeting to review progress with the new ground rules. Typically, some of the ground rules have worked well, but some may not have been functional and need modification.

Susanna's ground rule workshop

Check-in
- Going through the program and objectives
- Susanna asks everyone to comment on what they think about the workshop objectives

Clarifying
- Susanna asks participants to list most frustrating team behaviors individually
- Participants share behaviors in pairs, choose two, post and present
- Prioritising with 3 dots in pairs and presenting result

Solutions
- Susanna places people into small groups, and assigns each group one of the frustrating behaviors
- Groups write solutions for the challenges on flip-chart papers
- Rotating flip-chart papers every 5 minutes until all groups have given their ideas
- Prioritising in pairs with 10 stickers
- Checking that solutions are concrete
- Checking that group is committed by raising thumbs to vote

Action
- Susanna promises to follow-up on the ground rules in the next virtual team meeting.

Check-out
- Susanna asks participants to speak briefly about how they felt the workshop went.

In a virtual meeting setting, Susanna's process would not be very different than her format in the face-to-face setting. To clarify the challenging behaviours, she would ask the participants to list frustrating behaviours on the virtual whiteboard and to prioritise them. For solutions, instead of rotating flip-chart papers, she would invite participants to write solutions for the challenges one at a time on a shared virtual whiteboard. She would use a group prioritisation activity like dot-voting to have the group rank the challenges in order of importance.

BENEFITS, CHALLENGES AND APPLICATION OF A GROUND RULES WORKSHOP

Benefits
· Removes distractions so everyone can focus on their work
· Makes team cooperation easier

Challenges
· Be ready to deal with negative emotions. If there is an open conflict between team members about the way of working, you may need heavier tools than the Ground rules workshop.

Application
· Every team needs to agree on a way of working. However, the more the team needs to co-operate to get concrete results, the more important the ground rules become.

The ground rules workshop is a necessary activity for all teams. The more collaborative the team and working processes, the more important the ground rules become.

CHAPTER 9:

TEAM DEVELOPMENT: CELEBRATING SUCCESS

The end of the year is approaching which means that it is time for Susanna to come up with an activity for the team. In her mind, she imagines everyone bonding at a company picnic, and maybe lounging around a swimming pool together. In Susanna's perfect world, this is followed up with an energetic brainstorming session where her team comes up with goals for the upcoming year and makes plans on how to achieve them.

Unfortunately, reality is a bit different. Last year Susana organized a wine-tasting excursion for the entire team. After a long day of drinking, Susanna booked a motivational speaker for the team. Unfortunately, the motivational speaker's energy and enthusiasm were no match for the wine, and Susanna counted at least three separate people napping during the speech. Even worse, she could barely keep her eyes open herself! The year before was even worse. Susanna went too far in the other direction, and organized a day filled with presentations about the company, and new potential growth markets. She was hoping that providing coffee and donuts would cheer people up, but everyone carried themselves like a group of prisoners, looking at the window and waiting to be free. Susanna never managed to find the balance she wanted; to finish the year with something up-beat and fun, but still work related.

Susanna called her friend George and explained her dilemma. George did not hesitate in giving his answer "Susanna, you have to try success stories."

Susanna thought she knew where this was going, and she was not impressed. "George, I don't think you heard me. I already tried using a motivational speaker. The lady I brought in was droning on and on about success and giving examples of people rising from poverty to create million-dollar companies and so on, and my team looked like they were watching paint dry. They were bored to tears."

George laughed and said, "Well that is partly your fault. It is a novice mistake to force a group to listen to a speech after a day of wine tasting. But this activity is a little bit different. The success stories activity is all about the success the team has had together. It is a great way to get everyone feeling positive about the past year and at the same time it is a learning opportunity about how they can improve going forward."

Susanna was sold. *Success stories, that actually sounds pretty cool*, she thought. She was ready to give it a try.

This year the big night was scheduled to be held on December 15th. Susanna made sure to schedule the event before the Holidays began in full swing, and she decided to hold the festivities in a large conference room in the Fruit & Loading Inc. Headquarters in their London office. Most of the team was there, and some people even flew into London to make a long weekend out of it.

"It really is great to have all of you together again in the same room," began Susanna.

"And we're happy to be here. Now, isn't this the time for the wine?" Matt joked. At least, Susanna thought he was joking.

"Patience my friend, patience. We all are going to enjoy a very nice dinner together as a team. You can all thank our dear boss Bert for that. In fact, he will be joining us later for our celebration. But before we get to that, I want to reflect a bit on the year that we just completed together. What comes to mind when you think about it?"

Sarah Paige, Sales Leader for the Northern UK district shouted, "Changes. I think that the way we work now is very different than how we began the year."

Susanna nodded and thanked Sarah. "Nice observation, Sarah. I assume you are talking about positive changes, but one can never be sure. The focus of tonight's meeting is going to be completely positive. We are here to celebrate our successes. Let me tell you how."

Susanna began by giving out paper to her sales team. She asked each person to write down a personal example of success that they experienced at Fruit & Loading Inc last year and gave the group ten minutes to do so.

Matt did not seem entirely convinced. He transferred sales districts the past year and the adjustment had been difficult so far. He asked, "And what shall we write down if there are no positives? I could think and think, but I doubt I will come up with anything."

Susanna didn't let Matt continue any further. The meeting had to stay on a positive track.

"Then write down an example that you heard from someone else. Or something you observed somebody do. I know that some of you may feel a bit frustrated thinking back on how the year went, but I know for a fact that I experienced a moment of success with every single one of you."

Matt was still not convinced. "Try me," he challenged Susanna.

She paused and thought for a moment, and then grinned. "Remember our meeting we had in February when we first talked about your transfer to a new district? We had that meeting here in this office, and I remember that you were the first one of us to figure out how to use the Italian Espresso machine our client from Vienna sent us as a gift. The whole office was thrilled you figured it out!"

Matt laughed as he remembered struggling through the instruction manual and he agreed with Susanna that there was at least one success he could list.

"Any example of success, big or small, will do," Susanna said as a final instruction.

The room was quiet. People seemed to be thinking, but they weren't writing anything down. Susanna began to worry, but soon she relaxed. These things just take time and sometimes leaders must be patient. Gradually the participants began to write down their thoughts and Susanna watched them, satisfied. After ten minutes, she called time. "Split up into groups of three. Share the positive experiences you wrote down with each other."

Everyone was full of energy and excited to share their experiences. Susanna walked around the room and heard a variety of examples. Matt was talking about making his first sale in his new sales district, and how excited he was. "....I was used to selling thousands of pounds of apples weekly before, but my first sale in the new district for 500 apples made me the happiest of all!"

Susanna walked past Rita, Kevin, and Sarah's table and heard them talking about team co-operation in sales cases.

Susanna gave everyone a few more moments to exchange success stories before she called everyone back together and asked for volunteers to share stories with the entire group.

After each group had a chance to present a story that was shared, Susanna asked people to switch roles. Now, they were going to analyse their experiences to find out what created a feeling of success and reinvigorated their work.

"Now that we have had time to hear about successes that you all have enjoyed while working at Fruit & Loading Inc., it's time to think about them on a deeper level; what is the source of our success? Do your success stories share something in common? Think about this individually and write down anything you come up with."

Once everyone had been writing answers on their own for a while, Susanna asked them to steal ideas in groups of three.

She clarified a bit; "Yes, I said *steal*. Talk to your group and see what they came up with. If you like something, take it! This is an individual activity still. You are talking to others, but your aim is to collect the best ideas on your piece of paper."

The Sales Team found many positive things to say about their working community; the uncomplicated flow of information guaranteed seamless cooperation, the supervisors were always quick to motivate them with an encouraging word, and the coffee was always hot, strong, and easy to come by. Susanna shuffled the groups of three a few times, before she asked everyone to remain in their final groups and write down the best success factors on one piece of paper. Once everyone is done writing down success factors, Susanna instructed them to tape them to the wall.

When the last group had taped their paper to the wall, everyone stood up, gathered around, and read what had been produced.

"Hey, a lot of these are the same," observed Rita.

Each group had three ideas on average, but, many of the ideas were exactly the same. Susanna asked Rita to take a pen and cross off all the duplicates, and when she had finished there were just six success factors left.

"Do these ideas need to be presented?" asked Susanna.

All ideas seemed to be clear to the group because they had a chance to hear them again and again when they were busy stealing them from each other earlier.

Susanna was planning to have the group vote on what success factors were the most important, but after she saw the six ideas her Sales Team came up with, she decided that it was not necessary. The key success factors of the team were: persistence with clients, common goals, team collaboration, clear customer segmentation, positive and plentiful feedback, and virtual collaboration skills. Susanna was particularly happy about the last one.

Susanna didn't even need to ask for group feedback this time, as everyone began to chime in.

"I have the most fun at work when I work in a group. My team members are so entertaining, and I am always laughing," said Rita.

Sarah nodded in agreement, and added, how nice it is to work with a team full of individuals that share the same goals.

After the group had time to analyse their past successes, Susanna shifted the emphasis towards future solutions.

"OK everyone. There is something else I want you to think about before we end today's meeting. How can we turn these success factors into solutions for future work? I have written six success factors on separate posters hung on the walls. Your task is to walk around in silence and write down solutions using full clear sentences. And develop the ideas of others, too!"

Everyone started walking around and writing their ideas about how to increase success. Soon the walls were full of solutions. The scope and levels of seriousness varied, but almost all of them seemed to be practical.

"Everything you see written down on the posters are possible solutions you can take forward with you. There are a lot of them here, some easy to implement, while others may be a bit more ambitious. Your task is to choose your favourite ones and to design three bold steps that you are going to take to increase our success next year. *Bold* meaning something that makes a difference, and *step* meaning a concrete action point. You have five minutes on your own. Now the idea is to mix ambition with practicality."

After a short discussion on the meaning of 'bold' and a few jokes about Matt never being bold in his entire life, the group got into working. Susanna formed groups of three again and asked people to share and develop their bold action steps.

There was a lot to say, and Susanna saw that everyone had come up with a few actionable steps that they could use to create future successes based on what they had learned and achieved in the past. She was happy to see the group chatting without her needing to urge them to.

So much better than the motivational speaker, she thought. Just then, her phone began beeping frantically. It was company president Bert, who angrily informed her that he had been waiting for 20 minutes already at the restaurant bar.

Susanna called an end to the workshop and told the Sales Team that it was time to continue celebrating success at the restaurant with Bert. Susanna and the Team continued to enjoy a great end to the year, now armed with the tools to make the upcoming year an even better one.

ANALYSIS

Susanna began the success stories session using the familiar tool Me/ We/Us. She first framed the activity and gave an example of a success story, and then gave time for people to individually think of their own examples of success. If you would ask people to share success stories without giving them time to think, it would not be very successful. Time to think is essential.

After the Me stage, small groups were formed for sharing. Sharing in small groups is an easier transition from the Me stage, than a group-wide discussion would be. Finally, volunteers are asked to present a few examples to the whole group, but not too many. The energy level starts decreasing down after four or five stories are shared. Time management is key to hold a group's attention and maintain the positive atmosphere that the success stories activity creates.

Next, people begin to look for factors that are present in the success stories. What caused these things to happen? What factors are behind the events?

They started analysing their own examples of success and continued stealing ideas in groups of three. This process is called Idealogue. It is a highly effective communication tool that helps people create a shared reality of all ideas.

The Idealogue method

Stage 1: Individual stage
Participants are asked to write down their ideas in silence.

Stage 2: Steal with pride
At this stage, the facilitator introduces the ground rule and small groups of three are formed.
- Steal with Pride!
- Collect the best ideas on your own piece of paper.
- Share, listen, and develop ideas.

Stage 3: Repeated stealing
New groups of three are formed and the second stage is repeated several times.

**Stage 4:
Ideas selection**
At this stage, the participants remain in groups of three and select the best ideas.
- Choose the best ideas
- Try to reach consensus
- Write down best ideas on a piece of paper with a marker. (The number is not limited but best ideas cannot be many)
- One idea per paper
- When your group is ready post your ideas on the wall.

Stage 5: Ideas evaluation
The facilitator makes sure the group understands the posted ideas and the participants evaluate the results.

The solutions portion of the workshop used a method called gallery walk. It is a very simple method for collecting ideas, and unlike Idealogue, which can take 30 minutes to an hour, gallery walk is very quick to use. Gallery walk is a poor method for creating understanding and consensus because the participants do not communicate with each other. Susanna did not need to create group consensus in this case. Her aim was to create a pool of ideas which her team could use as they saw fit.

The Gallery walk

Questions are posted at stations around the room. Participants walk around the room in silence, composing answers to questions while reflecting upon and expanding on the answers given by others.

In the actioning section Susanna used Three bold steps. It has been said that 20 % of actions bring 80 % of the results. This is a way of saying that when it comes to making steps towards achieving a goal, it is quality over quantity. Susanna did not want her team to produce long lists of actions. She wanted them to focus on what can really make an impact. That is why she asked for only the actions that make a difference.

The structure of Susanna's Success Stories Workshop

Check-in
· Going through the program and objectives.
· Susanna asks everyone to give a short comment on what they think about workshop objectives.

Clarifying
· Susanna asks participants to individually write down and share success stories in small groups. The best stories are chosen and presented.
· Key success factors of the team are written down first individually and then developed in changing small groups of three. The best ideas are posted and prioritised.

Solutions
· Success factors are written on flipchart papers around the room. Groups write solutions for the success factors in silence.

Action
· Susanna asks participants to choose their favorite solutions and to write down three bold action steps.
· Action steps discussed and developed in small groups.

Check-out
· Susanna asks each participants to say one word how they felt the workshop went.

Using their success stories, the Sales Team figured out for themselves the reasons behind their success, and they had done it all in a positive environment. Interestingly, they had concentrated on success factors rather than analysing current problems. When people are reminded that they have succeeded in the past, this helps open the door for constructive dialogue and attitudes concerning difficult situations.

BENEFITS, CHALLENGES, AND APPLICATION OF SHARING SUCCESS STORIES WORKSHOP

Benefits

· Encourages positive thinking and energises the team
· People tend to remember results of positive workshops longer than results of problem-based workshops.
· Team development tool; created a great team atmosphere
· It is inspiring to talk about your own experiences.

Challenges

· Storytelling does not work if there are no personal experiences relating to the theme of the workshop.

Application

· Developing the team
· Ending the year, annual celebrations
· Reviewing or ending a project
· Developing sales

Susanna would have conducted this workshop almost the same way in a virtual meeting environment. The Me/We/Us activity would have worked fine. For the solutions stage, Susanna would have opened several whiteboards or simultaneous virtual chat rooms for discussion. Finally, the three bold steps activity could have been used efficiently using a shared virtual whiteboard.

CHAPTER 10:

THE PROGRESS MEETING

After the team development workshops, the Sales Team is working fantastically together. People are helping each other, and the proposed targets are being met with ease. Everyone is starting to get used to the new working environment, the travel ban, and updated sales targets. Fruit & Loading Inc. is a very pleasant place to be at the moment. Happy employees make for content customers, which lead to an overjoyed Bert.

A couple of weeks later, Bert has an idea that he runs by Susanna.

"The next quarterly meeting is coming up and I want to know how we are progressing with the new goals. Set up a virtual meeting with the Sales Team to give a status report."

Bert's genius surprises Susanna. *What an innovative thinker our boss has become, moving time consuming follow-up meetings online!* Susanna racks her brain, trying to think of a good name for this type of meeting. *I know that Bert expects to get a lot of information from the Sales Team…the best way to do this would be a lot of dynamic participation…* After a few moments of thought, Susanna decides to call this meeting *a progress meeting.*

When explaining to Susanna what he wants out of the meeting, Bert emphasises that the progress meeting should review approved changes in relation to company goals. Monthly discussions about goals help maintain the strategic course. Their goal is to check up on what has been successful and what hasn't, and listen to the group's solutions. Susanna takes all of this in and promises Bert that she will do her best.

After work, Susanna packs her favourite notebook and heads off to the city to think. She settles herself in a downtown café to work out the process of the meeting. She knows immediately that the structure of the meeting will be the usual one: check-in, clarifying the status, solutions, action, and check-out. Susanna also chooses warm-up and wind-down activities. While thinking about an appropriate method to deal with the actual content, Susanna has an epiphany: Force Field Analysis. She attended a course on it last autumn and had been waiting for the chance to try it out in a virtual environment.

The aim of Force Field Analysis is to analyse the current situation and identify any necessary changes. It is related to the commonly used SWOT analysis, and therefore participants often find it a familiar method of approaching the strategic goals.

The method feels especially appropriate now that the company has made big changes which are complicated to deal with and have caused the staff to worry, Susanna thinks.

The next day Susanna types an invite to the Sales Team. Susanna promises an efficient use of time and requests the participants to stay focused and find a quiet place to participate from.

CHECK-IN

Susanna has carefully prepared her presentation for the group of fifteen. She has chosen one-on-one interviews as a check-in tool, whereby participants pair up and discuss what should happen in the progress meeting. After a few minutes of discussion, the pairs go over their expectations with the whole group[*].

Please discuss expectations for today's meeting

3 minutes

Susanna's slide giving instructions for a one-on-one interview.

Then Susanna gives the participants a task to warm up their visual memories. She pulls up a PowerPoint slide that is covered with about a dozen seemingly unrelated pictures; a rubber duck, rainclouds, a symphony conductor, a roaring lion, and many more.

---

[*] It's easy to carry out one-on-one interviews on some platforms at just the click of a button, but others require that participants call each other or give out a conference telephone number to call. Either format is easy enough, but make sure all participants are comfortable and competent enough with the technology for this activity, and make sure to check the technology ahead of time yourself, so that you can be ready to help as needed.

"Everyone please take a moment to look at these pictures and decide which one best represents the mood that you are in right now. When you are ready, write your name on your favourite picture and share with the group why you chose it."

"I chose the melancholy looking guy walking along the beach on his own. I'm actually in quite a good mood, but I'm worried if closing down the two offices in St. Petersburg and Seville was the right decision," Kevin explains.

"I clicked on the spider because I'm concerned if we can really have a genuine discussion if the progress meetings are held virtually," says Minna.

"I chose the cup of coffee. I'm in a calm state of mind and I've even got a coffee cup here with me," assures Waldemar.

"I chose that picture of a Porsche. Let's get this sorted quickly, I'm in a rush to get to the airport!" Rita types.

"I chose that farmhouse because I'm looking forward to a trip at the weekend to my hometown in Cumbria," says Tony.

"Me too," says Billy. "That's why I chose that picture of the lake. After all, I am from The Lakes."

Force field analysis

Force field analysis is a management technique developed by Kurt Lewin for diagnosing situations. It is useful when looking at the variables involved in determining effectiveness and when planning and implementing change.

Lewin assumed that in any situation there are both driving and restraining forces that influence any change that may occur.

Force-Field-Analysis: STAGES

1) Write down positive and negative events; successes and challenges

2) Prioritise key development areas

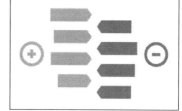

CLARIFYING: FORCE FIELD ANALYSIS

Susanna quickly goes through the day's agenda. Then she gets started and reviews the topic of the day, which she has summed up in the following question: What parts of the goal implementation have been successful, and which have proven to be challenging?

Before getting started, the group must first go through the solutions and actions decided on during the previous goal implementation workshop. Luckily Susanna has copied the notes from the whiteboard onto a PowerPoint slide. The group takes a minute to read the notes. Susanna uses Rita to help and tells her to say "done!" when she's read the page through.

"People tend to read at a similar speed so if one person gives a sign that they're done, the slideshow can advance at a suitable speed," Susanna explains after Billy asks why Rita decides how quickly the group reads.

Quiet reading ensues. Now and again Rita says, "done!", and George changes the page. At the end, Susanna shows a summary of the actions.

After going through the notes, Susanna asks the participants to write comments on the whiteboard about what has been successful so far. Susanna watches as interesting replies being appearing on the virtual whiteboard.

"Customers ended up being happier after we increased the number of customer visits."

"There is a good feeling at work. We are happier and do a better job completing our tasks and hitting our targets."

"We've found a new potential partner in Estonia."

Next the participants write current areas for development of the goals on the virtual whiteboard. As they write, Susanna notices that some of the text is showing up very small, or in a colour which is hard to read. To help the process along, she writes the text again on the same line, so that the participants will be able to see each other's comments. A skilled facilitator doesn't let weak spots in virtual platforms get in their way.

Around ten topics are listed. Then Susanna explained to the group that it is now time to decide which of these is most important. As usual, she gave her team the chance to vote on it.

"Everyone has three Xs which they can place next to developmental points that should be discussed today. Now choose where to put them!" Susanna says, encouraging the group.

Susanna's aim is to have them select two or three topics, so that the group can be split up into smaller groups where the selected topics will be discussed. The Xs end up spanning three ideas;

1. *Maintaining strong growth*
2. *Streamlining operations*
3. *Increasing employee happiness.*

Susanna writes them down on the virtual whiteboard and decides that now would be the perfect time to pause the meeting and give everyone a 15-minute coffee break.

CONSIDERING SOLUTIONS AND SELECTING SOLUTIONS

During the break Susanna munches on a sandwich, but she's nervous and unable to enjoy her coffee, something that is very rare for her. After the break she intends to run her first ever virtual Open Space meeting. She had used the Open Space method plenty in face-to-face meetings, but she was worried how the free flowing, multi-group activity would translate virtually. Luckily the group returns in a timely manner and even Minna in Tokyo had time for some sushi. Susanna knows from experience that you need an energising activity after lunch to jumpstart the energy levels and brainpower of the team while they digest. After reading the nice comments written in chat when everyone returned from lunch ("A virtual workday is more effective than real life ones", "I just had the best chocolate milkshake ever!") Susanna put the group through a quick mental workout before the meeting starts again.

"You have 30 seconds to write some words on the whiteboard using the letters SETIBLMO. This is a competition," Susanna reveals to the team.

"Impossible," snorts Minna.

Waldo, unlike Minna, produces 'limes', 'slot', 'bite', 'mob', 'mobs' and 'let' in the thirty seconds and Susanna congratulates Waldo on his performance which largely outshone everyone else.

Bert is missing, he hasn't commented in the chat.

"Mr. Upper-Thrapplewaite!" shouts Susanna. She is not answered. "Bert!" Susanna yells down the phone.

"Yes, what is it?" Bert answers, surprised.

He had forgotten all about the chat function and had been waiting patiently on the line with his phone muted. Susanna notes that in the future even trivial instructions should be written for everyone to see on a shared slide. During the break the people might have something completely different on their mind which makes it easy to forget small details once the meeting resumes.

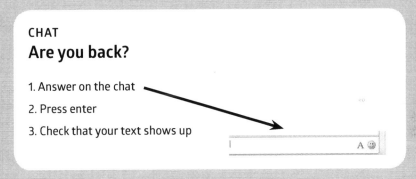

The 'Break over' slide.

Susanna begins by telling the participants how solutions are created through teamwork.

"You all remember the Open Space method from the development event last year. Now we're going to use the same method but with a slight change. We have already selected three areas: strong growth, streamlined operations, and employee happiness. A leader will be chosen for each area. The leader is responsible for making sure that the best possible solutions are found for their assigned area. In the next phase of the meeting, a concrete plan of action will be made from the solutions. The participants' task is to pool their skills for use by the leaders, and, if necessary to move from one meeting to another to help the leaders of each assigned area. Each of you can choose which group to participate in."

The Open Space method

Open Space is a self-organising meeting method that allows many topics to be discussed simultaneously.

· Each topic has a meeting with a chairperson responsible for running and documenting the meeting.
· Participants may freely move from one meeting to another.

"What if you don't have any skills to pool?" asks Margaret.

"Choose the topic you can give the most to. And if you really don't have anything to give at all, you don't have to participate," Susanna says. She knows that Margaret will participate and contribute to all the topics anyway.

Susanna opens three different whiteboards and asks for volunteers to lead the meetings*. Kevin enthusiastically volunteers to lead the growth group.

"It's brilliant that I'm in this group, though I would have had something to offer in the happiness issue, too. Can I leave my own meeting if I want to work on a different topic?"

"If you want to leave you can, but you need to delegate the leadership of your meeting to someone else," Susanna advises.

John, happily thinking about the larks and happy birds mentioned in Minna's vision statement, decides to volunteer to lead the happiness meeting. Bert is nominated as leader for the streamlined operations meeting, but he declines due to his managerial role and instead suggests Margaret. As Margaret hesitates out of shyness, Rita volunteers.

Susanna is satisfied. She makes a note of the meeting topics, the names of the leaders and the telephone numbers for each meeting conference room on the whiteboard. The meetings can begin.

The groups begin working, filling the whiteboards with texts, pictures and drawings. Susanna has time to take a breather. She goes to get a cup of coffee and returns to the groups to check how they are doing and if everything is fine, in regard to both the technology and the participants. She reminds the participants of the time and encourages them to write down as much as they can.

Susanna receives a message from John, who is leading the happiness group. The group hasn't managed to get to grips with the happiness theme and is finding it hard to come up with solutions. Susanna gives them some advice.

---

* In some virtual platforms, the division of a group into group work spaces is extremely easy. The calls are transferred automatically, and the whiteboard is ready and waiting. Most technologies allow the facilitator to open several whiteboards or sessions, but the sound input, or conference call for each must be set up separately. It can require a little perseverance and fiddling with controls, but it is well worth it.

"It's good to first start with obstacles, for example things that prevent employees from being happy. Then the group can consider solutions."

Margaret is first to find an obstacle.

"I don't speak for everyone, but I know that my happiness is threatened by those old decrepit chairs Headquarters' kitchen..."

The meetings continue on. An hour and a half after the task started Susanna signals to the participants that they now have half an hour to prioritise the best solutions. When the time is up, Susanna invites the group back to the meeting and brings up the growth group's whiteboard first.

"Everything is clear, and even prioritised a bit," says Kevin from the growth group. Susanna takes a look at the group's solutions. Under Kevin's leadership the group came up with many ready-to-use suggestions for the export of organic British apples around the world.

Susanna opens the group's whiteboards one by one and guides the participants in prioritising the best solutions by putting them in order from best to worst.

"Everyone marks the best solution with the number one, the second-best with the number two, and the third best with the number three."

AGREEING ON ACTIONS

"We have now found solutions. Now we're going to solidify the actions. Think of the steps that need to be taken to execute the solutions. Who is going to do what? And when? This is what you need to think about. We're going to work in the same way as we did before and with the same leaders. I've opened three whiteboards and the aim is to write down concrete steps you propose to take in accordance with each topic."

The groups get to work.

Actioning stage with open space technology

There can be several simultaneous topics
(3–10 depending on the size of the group).

Roles
The leader is responsible for making a concrete action plan for the best solutions: who, what, when.

The participant familiarises herself or himself with the meetings' solutions and helps the leader solidify actions. Participants can choose which group they participate in.

Starting
The meeting begins once the topics, places and leadership responsibilities are given out.

Ending
To end, all the actions are examined together. It is good to visualise them on a shared action map, for example.

The time is up and the day is nearly over. The groups successfully produced actions which could be taken to achieve the development topics.

Susanna still wants to check how committed the participants are to the actions the groups suggested. She instructs the participants to use the virtual polling tool, which allows everyone to vote at the click of a mouse.

"On a scale of one to five, please answer the following: 'I am committed to our team's actions.'"

Susanna is surprised to see scattered results. There are lots of fives and a few fours, but Bert has given a one and Margaret has voted two. Susanna's mouth goes dry. If the leader himself isn't at all committed to action, the entire strategy is in danger. She asks Bert and Margaret needs to change in order for them to give a high score.

Margaret is quick to answer, saying that she has been assigned too many tasks.

"If I have to do this much, I'm going to resign straight away!" she says up front.

Bert steps in, as he sees that some of the tasks assigned to Margaret are clearly financial manager Robson's duties. Margaret calms down and gives a three. At the same time, Bert realises he had understood the scale wrong. He had wanted to give the best possible number, and before Susanna has time to worry, Bert clicks on five.

Everything is fine. At her desk, Susanna breathes a sigh of relief.

CHECK-OUT

"We've arrived at the final stage of the meeting. I would like everyone to leave a brief comment on how we did. Please write in the chat if you want to say what's on your mind."

Some people began making small talk, discussing what they were going to have for lunch, while others began to write down feedback about how the meeting went. As Susanna waited, the screen began to fill up.

It's great to get things moving forward and it would be brilliant if there was a facilitator at live meetings too.

We had a three-hour session and there were no technical problems at all. Now there's an achievement.

I'm surprised it's possible to hold a meeting this long virtually, and even get results out of it faster than you would with a normal meeting.

The virtual meeting required us to learn a little bit, but it was definitely worth it.

To close the meeting, Susanna shows the participants a decorative slide filled with a big smiling emoji, and the words *Thank you for today!*

"Once again, thanks to each and every one of you for your contributions today. This type of effort and participation is what makes successful meetings possible. I hope you all realize how valuable it is."

With those kind words, Susanna ended the meeting and dismissed everyone.

ANALYSIS AND REFLECTION

Susanna is tired after the progress meeting. They had covered some big issues, and Susanna had prepared for disputes and for deviation from the schedule. She decides to take the afternoon off to go to her favourite café to review what happened in the meeting. Susanna feels that there was some success, as the group engaged in lots of discussion and produced concrete actions. The solutions were further refined; a roadmap of action points was made, and the stage is set for further development in future meetings.

As Susanna is navigating London traffic while on her way to the café, Bert calls.

"Susanna, hi! You were so good that I'm going to take you to the best restaurant in the city. You've got time, don't you?"

Susanna doesn't object but asks Bert to give her an hour to freshen up.

About an hour and a half later, seated at the swanky French restaurant *La Pomme*, Bert orders the best house champagne instead of his trademark apple cider. He smiles, and addresses Susanna.

"Listen, I was just going over some calculations and I've noticed that your virtual facilitation has already saved the company tens of thousands. If we keep this up and average twelve monthly virtual meetings, as well as continue to conduct development events and discussions virtually, we can save at least one hundred thousand dollars a year!"

Susanna blushes at Bert's praise and grins. Bert continues with something else that surprises Susanna.

"And you deserve a bonus and raise," Bert exclaims, and hands Susanna an envelope labelled *Bonus*.

"I've just read up about the methods..." Susanna mumbles modestly. She doesn't dare open the envelope straight away, and quickly puts it safely away in her purse.

"Never mind modesty, Susanna, this is excellent! With your help, we've saved the company from another round of cutbacks."

The colleagues take their time in the restaurant, chatting for once about something other than work; surfing, white beaches, and tropical weather.

Susanna processes the methods of facilitation subconsciously. She begins to believe in herself. Perhaps the future really does lie in virtual group work methods!

When the weekend arrived, Susanna wanted to have a chat about facilitation. She invites her facilitator friend George over for a glass of wine and some French cheese.

"Bert's real moment of genius was linking the progress meetings to goal implementation. Before, the group used to bring all kinds of presentations and issues to meetings. The meetings were spent chatting for hours about employees' birthday presents and the length of coffee breaks. Usually the topics didn't apply to everyone and weren't open to discussion or group consensus, either. The implementation of the goals is the most important goal, and it applies to everyone. In the future, all our monthly meetings will be progress meetings which will monitor the progress of our goals. The Sales Team can decide on other matters using some other forum," affirms Susanna, as she begins to explain the structure of her meeting to George.

THE STRUCTURE OF A PROGRESS MEETING

CHECK-IN

"Like any meeting type, I started with a check-in activity. I tried to give the group a check-in activity that would direct their focus towards the task at hand; the meeting. So I placed them into pairs and told them to interview each other about their ideas and thoughts for the meeting."

George nodded knowingly. "Ah yes. I understand what you did there, Susanna. But don't you think that a discussion of the meeting expectations might be a bit heavy for an opening activity? It is good to sometimes ease people into the flow of a meeting by playing a game or engaging the group by using a silly warm-up activity."

"That's what I did next. I showed everyone a slide with different pictures on it; a tornado, a gas station, umbrella, rainbow...a bunch of seemingly random things. Then, I had people select a picture that represented their attitude towards the meeting. This activity lightened the mood, but at the same time it made people summarize what they had just discussed in pairs; the expectations for the meeting. After everyone had a chance to relate their thoughts and emotions to a picture, everyone was on the same page and the group's expectations for the day were coordinated."

"Very good," George says encouragingly. "I am glad to see the check-in phase become a habit for you. All meetings need this phase to get people dialled in and paying attention. It also is a good way to pass the time while everyone gets settled in, but I am sure you already know this."

Susanna smiles and nods in agreement about the importance of a good check-in phase before continuing on to the next phase.

CLARIFYING

"It's important to show the current situation after beginning the meeting. Here I used Force Field Analysis for the clarifying stage."

"Ah, the good old Force Field Analysis!" George is already enthusiastic, and they haven't even chilled the wine yet.

Susanna elaborates.

"First we reviewed the goals and checked where we succeeded and where we faced challenges. Then we chose the most current challenges, which clearly require some thought."

George nods at his friend proudly. Susanna has become quite the virtual facilitation expert. George can imagine the Fruit & Loading Inc. Sales Team awarding the best grades for management and motivation at work in the next company wellbeing survey. Nothing is more rewarding for team members than to participate in decision making and present their own ideas for change and doing so in a positive working atmosphere.

"Force Field Analysis is an excellent tool for clarifying the current situation."

The friends grab a wine bottle from the fridge. Sipping her cool drink, Susanna relaxes and intuitively senses that Bert has at least ten new visions up his sleeve about how the group could hang out virtually and how the company could become the world's best with the help of Susanna 's virtual facilitation skills.

SOLUTIONS AND ACTION

Susanna used a variation of a group discussion tool called Open Space twice in her workshop; once to think of solutions and then once more to think of specific actionable steps. The Open Space tool that Susanna used let people decide which questions they want to talk about. They also could move freely between the sub-meetings if they got bored of one aspect and wanted to contribute elsewhere. This type of tool lets people fully realize their potential; the individual is in complete control in regard to what they talk about and how they contribute.

In the goal implementation workshop Susanna also used a method for dealing with many simultaneous questions called Café. In the Café method the facilitator systematically rotated the people around the questions. This way each participant will understand and contribute to each question. That was very important because everyone needs to be committed for goals to be successfully implemented.

Progress meetings are a bit different than goal implementation workshops. These meetings deal with practical questions that are not equally important to everyone, or perhaps not important at all to some. The aim of these meetings is not to look for commitment, but for practical solutions and concrete action. The Open Space Technology allows participants to self-organise and to allocate their resources better. This is very efficient especially when you have many questions that require expert knowledge.

The structure of Susanna's virtual progress meeting

Pre-Meeting
· Sending invitations to participants.

Check-in
· Going through program and objectives.
· One-on-one interviews (pair discussion) about expectations for the day.
· Visual memory warm-up: choose a picture from the slide that best captures your feelings about the session.

Clarifying
· Participants write successes and challenges simultaneously on whiteboard.
· Prioritising key challenges.

Solutions
· Many simultaneous meetings. Each meeting has a leader, others move freely.

Action
· Many simultaneous meetings. Each meeting has a leader, others move freely. Goal is to agree on concrete steps for each meeting; what, who, when.

Check-out
· Group discussion and feedback about the meeting and resulting decisions and actions stemming from the meeting.

CHECK-OUT

Susanna thanks George and thinks about the final phase of her meeting, check-out. Here she wants to get at least one comment from each participant. By having everyone share at least one comment, the whole group gets a sense of achievement, participation, and closure. While the check-out phase can be brief and not as complex or heavy as other meeting phases, Susanna knows that the importance of it cannot be forgotten, and she ends all meetings, regardless of the type, with some sort of check-out phase.

In face-to-face meetings Susanna's tools and way of working would not be very different from a virtual meeting. In face-to-face meetings Susanna prefers to give lots of time for individual thinking and pair discussions. That would be particularly apparent in the clarifying stage and Susanna would have the team members first think individually of successes and challenges. Susanna believes individual thinking always brings depth into ideas. Second, she would have pairs discuss and choose ideas. When discussing ideas, they become clearer and they are easier to prioritise.

The structure of a face-to-face progress meeting

Check-in
- Going through program and objectives.
- One-on-one interviews (pair discussion) about expectations for the day. Ask participants to write and post expectations. Make sure the expectations are relevant.

Clarifying
- Participants write successes and challenges on their own
- Pair discussion and each pair chooses and presents two key successes and challenges.
- Take out the duplicates before prioritising.
- Prioritising key challenges. Participants sign the challenges they want to solve today.

Solutions
- Many simultaneous meetings for creating solutions for prioritised challenges. Each meeting has a leader, others move freely.

Action
- Many simultaneous meetings. Each meeting has a leader, others move freely. Goal is to agree on three bold steps for each meeting; what, who, when.

Check-out
- Group discussion and feedback about the meeting, resulting decisions and actions stemming from the meeting.

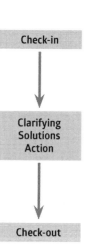

What was the key point in this chapter? For many companies a progress meeting involves the meeting chairman addressing specific teams or individuals while everyone else waits for their turn to be addressed. Most participants are bored and wait for their turn to speak. Meeting participants also may have the chance to suggest solutions, but they do not have true decision-making power.

BENEFITS, CHALLENGES AND APPLICATION OF THE PROGRESS MEETING

Benefits
- Helps team members – including the leader – to see and understand the current situation
- Makes it easy to deal with barriers to high performance
- Supports goal attainment
- Saves time, instead of talking to each employee one at a time, you deal with challenges of all team members at once.
- Allows team members to collaborate and align activities

Challenges
- Time consuming

Application
- Excellent meeting structure to review progress of practically anything
- Reviewing and energising changes and goals
- Structure can be applied for weekly or monthly meetings
- One of the very key activities in creating and maintaining high performance

Progress meetings are versatile and can be used in monthly meetings, or special workshops.

In Susanna's progress meeting all participants wrote down their successes and challenges. In five minutes the situation of the team was clear to everyone. With her way of working Susanna opened the eyes of all participants and invited them to take responsibility. When the team members understood the situation, they were able to design complex solutions requiring co-operation without the intervention of the leader.

The progress meeting is an effective tool that creates continuous improvement. This workshop helps you refocus your team and achieve better results!

CHAPTER 11:

THE SIX KEYS TO FACILITATING SUCCESSFUL VIRTUAL MEETINGS

When people meet and are able to interact as a group, information is shared, and the individual become more knowledgeable. That is why this book repeatedly emphasizes the importance of meetings; every meeting is an opportunity to create a focused, connected and motivated team. Meetings are ultimately a product of the people that participate in them. A group of very bright and eager people can overcome dull or flawed meeting formats to spend productive time together. On the other hand, a group of overworked, underpaid, uninterested and unmotivated employees may struggle no matter what meeting format is used. However, there are keys and techniques that form the building blocks of successful meetings, and throughout this book Susanna has used them in both virtual and face-to-face meeting environments. This chapter is dedicated to virtual meetings, since virtual meetings are less familiar for many, and tend to be more of a challenge.

It is easy to think that if a technique works in a face-to-face meeting then it will also work in a virtual meeting. This is only partially true. The tools that we have seen Susanna use work in both face-to-face and virtual meeting environments. The difference is that virtual meetings are more difficult to lead due to some challenges that simply do not exist in a face-to-face meeting environment.

First off, people behave differently in a virtual environment than they may in a face-to-face meeting. Susanna's experience shows that in regular face-to-face meetings, less rules are needed, and people participate more willingly. They do not need as much specific instruction or encouragement. People are also more accountable in face-to-face meetings just by being in the same room together. Most people want to avoid appearing rude by not listening or by blatantly doing something else while another person is talking, so they tend to pay attention. Compare this to virtual meetings, where participants are often muted and not visible to anyone else. There are a million ways to be off-track virtually. I have found that a lot of the time, people sometimes get distracted with the best of intentions; they might try to multi-task by catching up on work emails during a virtual presentation. Or, they might be trying to catch virtual Pokémon while listening to their manager talk about a new vision statement. Whatever their intentions may be, there is a much lower degree of accountability in virtual environments.

Secondly, leading successful virtual meetings requires much more preparation that face-to-face meetings do. Susanna was a decisive leader who commanded the attention of the group by giving clear instructions and transitioning smoothing from one phase of the meeting to the next. But for her to pull this off, she needed to invest more time into content creation and structuring her virtual meetings.

Besides these challenges, there are huge advantages that virtual meetings have over face-to-face meetings. People are more realistic and candid in virtual meetings and are more likely to stand their ground and fight for their opinions rather than blindly following and agreeing with something just for the sake of agreement. The virtual format also seems to reduce ego, which makes meetings more about the content, and less about personalities.

Susanna has noticed six key practices that lead to successful virtual and face-to-face meetings; setting ground rules, explicitly identifying the different roles people take during the meeting (facilitator, partici-pant, presenter, etc.), activating participants, using group memory, dividing participants into small groups, and preparing the technology.

1. Set ground rules for virtual meetings
2. Identify different roles – especially the facilitator
3. Activate participants
4. Use group memory
5. Divide participants into small groups
6. Prepare and check the technology

The best practises for leading dynamic meetings.

Adopting these practices and using them regularly in meetings makes a virtual facilitator's job much easier; there is less stress, fewer technical difficulties and participants relax.

1. SET GROUND RULES

Think back to your first day of school; the smell of fresh books, small desks, new friends, and new rules. Yes, rules. Chances are, the first thing your teacher did once they managed to get everyone seated and attentive, was outline the class rules. Giving schoolchildren clear, understandable rules helps outline acceptable behaviour. Virtual meetings are the same. Hopefully your meeting attendees are easier to control than a group of primary schoolchildren, but they need rules as well. By outlining clear rules for virtual meeting attendees, you ensure that you will not be surprised by unexpected behaviour during the meeting.

Agreeing on and sticking to a set of ground rules is even more important when participants aren't physically in the same location and therefore can't see each other. Stricter rules are needed as to how group members are expected to participate and what they are and are not allowed to do. Susanna gives an example.

"Our Sales Team has worked together for years at Fruit & Loading Inc. Nevertheless, not everyone recognises everyone else's telephone voice, at least not all of the time. Once there was an embarrassing episode when Minna Adams checked into a virtual meeting when she was travelling and feeling a little under the weather with a cold. She sounded so muffled that someone mistook her for Bert! No one could recognize her voice and after she was called Bert, she was embarrassed, and the entire meeting got a bit off-track."

The less participants know each other, the more important it is that people say their own name before speaking. This way there is no confusion. Stating ones' name before speaking also avoids situations when people begin to talk over each other. It also calms and prepares the other participants to listen to what the speaker has to say.

Susanna's favourite virtual meeting practice is called 100 % participation. This means that people attending the meeting must give 100 % of their attention to what is happening in the meeting. They need to actively be listening to who is speaking and to what is being said. No one can check their emails, look through customer contacts, or live chat with customers. In physical face-to-face meetings, this rule does not need explaining as it would be considered very rude and potentially damaging to ones' career if they were to pull out their phone and read the news in front of the rest of the company during an important meeting. But virtually it is different. Many people use the internet with multiple windows open and technology is geared towards multitasking. This means that this rule should be explicitly explained, more than once.

"During my meetings, no-one leaves or returns without first notifying the others. If something urgent comes up and you have to leave, you must let everyone else know."

Focused participation also helps eliminate background noise. In order to be 100% focused and tuned into a meeting, participants should find a quiet place from which to attend. There is always background noise in public places. For example, if you're waiting for a train, not only is there lots of background noise but it is a task in itself and will definitely prevent you from actively participating.

"A while ago, Billy Campbell happened to have a business trip scheduled at the same time as a virtual meeting. He decided to participate from the airport while waiting for his flight. Though he was in a quiet place, you could hear passenger announcements and all of the other travellers passing by. Luckily he muted the phone for the majority of the time, but Billy wasn't properly focused, and the other participants picked up on it," Susanna remembers.

Ground rules and clear instructions are also needed before any issue is opened up for group discussion. How do you, as the meeting leader, want the group to discuss something? How much time do you wish to spend on this discussion? Imagine if you ask a group of twenty to decide on something in a virtual meeting without giving the group any guidance. You need a clear set of ground rules to prevent chaos and keep the group on track.

Some of the ground rules Susanna uses to create the right expectations for the meeting. One of her ground rules is virtual patience. Sometimes batteries run out, a connection fails, or software just doesn't work. She can be facilitating a meeting and her internet connection could cut out for ten minutes. But Susanna has hardly ever been in a situation where the virtual meeting couldn't be followed through right to the end. With this ground rule Susanna wants to create trust that despite all small problems the participants should not worry, they are part of the virtual game and the meeting will be followed through by any means necessary.

2. IDENTIFY AND ASSIGN DIFFERENT ROLES: USING A FACILITATOR

The definition of a facilitator is someone who leads a meeting by focusing only on the process of the meeting, and who is neutral towards the content. It is impossible to concentrate on the content and simultaneously guide the process successfully. Often, the person leading the meeting becomes caught up in the content, defends his or her own ideas and no longer notices what's going on around them. Susanna has read that the chair of a meeting typically talks for 70 % of the time and while talking, is unable to combine his or her own knowledge with the knowledge of the rest of the group. That means that the chair cannot put the realisations or solutions that come up during the meeting into use, or help the group make decisions. Using a facilitator who is removed from the content solves this problem.

The role of a facilitator in both face-to-face and virtual meetings is to lead a meeting in a neutral manner and to concentrate on the meeting as a process. Someone who focuses purely on group working methods does wonders for physical meetings, not to mention virtual meetings, where technology poses its own challenges. A planned process led by a facilitator in a virtual environment is a must for staying on schedule and ensuring that everyone concentrates fully on participation.

There are other essential roles for a successful meeting. A *presenter* explains the content to be examined during a meeting to the participants. The participants then share their own ideas.

In virtual meetings it's also good to make have a *technical support person*, who can help participants with technical problems while the facilitator continues leading the meeting. The leader of the meeting can also assign the role of a *secretary*, who records the meeting notes, and then distributes it to the participants.

3. ACTIVATE PARTICIPANTS

Without passion and enthusiasm, nothing worthwhile gets done. This generally holds true for meetings as well, and it applies equally to the meeting leader, and the meeting attendees. If the person running the meeting does not seem interested and engaged by the material and setting, how can the participants be? It is crucial to lead meetings in an engaging, purposeful way. Have a plan and confidently follow that plan. Be decisive in guiding the group through the agenda. Properly structuring the meeting agenda is crucial. If there is a long presentation, the group will need a break afterwards. Even half an hour of focused listening to a presentation is a long time. To get a group to refocus, Susanna learned a series of simple activation tools to motivate the group. Some excellent tools are the use of smileys and voting icons, polling, drawing and writing. These techniques are used to not just check the focus level of the group, but to refocus them and bring attention levels back up to where the facilitator or meeting leader wants them.

When leading a meeting, it is a recommended format to have a dynamic activity to start the meeting. This can be a game to get people thinking or some sort of conversation in small groups to get people talking with one another.

After the group is activated, the meeting leader can proceed with the agenda and monitor the groups' attention level. If people seem to be getting impatient or distracted, a short break, or another activity can be given to right the ship.

4. USING GROUP MEMORY

Using group memory is a key part of facilitation. Group memory functions as a mechanism for storing the ideas produced during a meeting or brainstorming session. By recording ideas and presenting them to the group, discussion is produced. Simply put, group memory means that issues important to the group are written down and made visible to participants. In doing so, no ideas are neglected or forgotten, and conversation is enhanced. People can only remember a few things at a time, and the visual aid of writing everything down becomes an extension of the mind. This extension of the mind is the group's memory.

By writing down all the ideas produced together, the original owner of the idea, the person that thought of it, is made irrelevant and the ideas can stand on their own. The idea has become property of the group.

If the group voices issues and makes comments and they are taken into account as someone writes them down for others to see – on a virtual whiteboard, for example – the issues are shared with the group. It's also easier for participants to get involved and make progress if they feel as though they are being heard. Writing things down lightens the atmosphere during disputes and when dealing with difficult subjects. Groups are also better able to resolve conflict if things are written down. When sensitive issues are recorded, they are less personal, and participants tend to be more objective.

"Bert gave me permission to purchase some video conferencing equipment. While I was checking out the technology, I noticed that the video equipment didn't contain any feature that would allow me to write down participants' ideas in a group memory space so that they could be prioritised and decided on in front of everyone. The focus of the meeting would be lost entirely if I use this equipment!" Susanna thought it best to leave the expensive equipment alone. If she had to choose between a video conference where everyone could be seen, and the option to use group memory, then the decision is an easy one. Group memory wins every time.

5. USE SMALL GROUPS AND BE AWARE OF GROUP DYNAMICS

Susanna finds the use of small groups to a very important activation method. If the size of a group becomes too large, it is common for only a few participants to actively participate while most of the group listens... or pretends to listen. The energy level decreases dramatically when there are over fifteen people in a group. While it is true that more people in a group means more resources to draw from, the group's focus, energy level, and the collective intelligence of the group decreases when it becomes too large. When thoughts and ideas are first refined together in a small group, they are often better formed than individual opinions. Small groups can be used to consider expectations, to consider individual actions after a group decision has been made, or at the end of a meeting. Also, in smaller groups or pairs, it's easier for participants to express themselves without the pressure of speaking in front of a large group.

In a virtual meeting, even five members in a small group can be enough to affect energy levels. Susanna always splits larger groups into small groups, finding that three seems to be the 'magic number'.

6. PREPARE YOURSELF, AND THE TECHNOLOGY

Susanna is quite an experienced facilitator. In fact, when it comes to planning meetings she's even slightly revolutionary.

"Meetings everywhere would be saved if only people would prepare for them properly. If you think more about what you want to achieve during the meeting, on what schedule and how, people participating in the meetings would have clear direction, and as the goals of the meeting are achieved the group's mind-set would improve. This would lead to work that is more effective and innovative. Progress would be made, all the while reducing frustration and feelings of uselessness."

In fact, a large part of facilitation is advance preparation, which becomes even more important in a virtual setting. The cornerstones of preparation for virtual meetings are planning and scheduling the process, selecting tools and planning your presentation, and being familiar with the technology. Susanna's meeting process typically consists of three stages; clarifying, solutions and action. Each stage consists of creating and choosing ideas and Susanna needs to choose the way of working. For instance, in the progress meeting during the clarifying stage the participants first listed successes and challenges on whiteboard and second, the participants chose key challenges by writing three X's next to their personal key obstacles. After choosing the way of working, she decides how to facilitate the beginning, energisers, breaks and ending.

Finally, she checks the timing of the meeting. Do the planned activities fit the window of time given? Is there enough time to allow for extra questions, breaks, and other unexpected delays like people arriving late, or a technological mishap?

Reserving enough time for the workshop is crucial. Most of the three stage workshops in this book can be facilitated in three and a half hours or less. Virtual workshops tend to require less time, roughly an hour less on average for a three-stage workshop. Perhaps virtual workshops take less time because people are more focused, and people can organize in new groups much more quickly virtually, than they can in reality.

Dear reader, I already hear you complaining that all of this preparation and three-stage workshops take much longer to execute than your normal meetings do. This is true, but as a result your entire team will be more committed and have a better understanding of the content covered in these workshops. The end result is employees that are capable of self-organizing their work. Remember how Susanna focused on quality over quantity regarding the action points her team commits to? The same is true for meetings. Organizing a quality meeting takes more time, , but you will need to hold them less often, they will be more engaging and more effective than the meetings you currently hold.

Susanna's way of planning a meeting or workshop

1. Choosing stages

2. Choosing the way of working for each stage
3. Planning the beginning, breaks, energisers, and ending of the meeting
4. Checking the time schedule

In addition to choosing the best processes, methods and activation tools, Susanna also makes sure to check that the technology being used actually is capable of executing her plan. Does it have the options needed for dividing the group into small groups, each with their own chat room? Does it have built in activation activities? By checking the technology herself, she becomes very familiar with it and can quickly solve any problems that may occur during the meeting.

Whenever she finds herself breaking out into a sweat over a technical difficulty, Susanna repeats a mantra to herself; *you can never completely know the technology.*

In practice, good technical skills bring stability to the meeting. Nevertheless, a facilitator doesn't need to be a computer guru. The best way to ensure technical reliability is to prepare for any possible risks in advance by making back-up plans for the various components of the meeting. Susanna realised the importance of back-up plans while she was facilitating a meeting where Britain's Foreign Trade Minister was participating.

"That very same day that our virtual platform had stopped working and I had to use an application which was different from the one I'd planned to use. Luckily, I had decided in advance to take along a member of the technical support staff and to think of an alternative application as a back-up plan. Instead of having to cancel the whole meeting, we were able to set up a second platform, and the start of the meeting was only delayed by fifteen minutes."

To prevent batteries from running out, computers from breaking, and facilitators from having to leave the meeting, it's a good idea to think about bringing along back up equipment. Extra batteries, an extra laptop, and even an extra facilitator who can fill in for you if you get a bout of the hiccups are things to think about.

One of Susanna's best practices is the technical check-in that participants carry out in advance before their first virtual meeting. Technical problems usually arise because of firewalls, pop-up blockers or other technical challenges. If at the start of a meeting fifteen participants are on the line and three of them are experiencing technical difficulties, the facilitator can find it hard to solve everyone's problems at the same time, and the other participants can become frustrated with waiting. That's why it's better to carry out the technical check-in the day before.

We have gone through the best practices for virtual collaboration. They are also the best practices for face-to-face meetings. Is there any difference? Yes, in the difficult virtual world where participants do not see each other and where technical challenges can lurk around every corner, they become even more important.

CHAPTER 12:

SYSTEMATIC LEADERSHIP AND BOOSTING TEAM PERFORMANCE

We started the book discussing facilitative leadership; the participatory practice of guiding the group process with all participants at the same time in one place. People accept and adapt to change more rapidly in group situations, for example a weekly meeting when everyone is present and interacting with each other. Think about how long an idea or cultural change would take if it had to be spread individually, one person at a time... It sometimes resembles a game of Telephone where there is a risk of original message being completely distorted and losing meaning by the time it travels throughout the organisation.

Susanna, quite the planner, has systematically and consciously organised her leadership activities using tools that must be familiar to you by now.

Susanna's leadership activities

· Kickoff meeting
· Goal implementation workshop
· Coaching
· Problem solving workshop
· Offers and needs negotiations
· Stakeholder analysis with communication plan
· Ground rules
· Celebrating success
· Progress meeting

It can be overwhelming trying to make sure you use all of these activities, but there is a tool for that too; the annual cycle.

ANNUAL CYCLE

Susanna structures her meetings very carefully. Every process is carefully ordered with the aim of getting the most out of the group. Her yearly schedule is also planned and ordered to maximize results.

One of the first things Susanna does every year is the kickoff meeting. Susanna holds a kickoff meeting to get her team to accept and act on any new goals. This is exactly what the kickoff meeting tries to achieve; it informs the participants of the new goals and it also helps people to understand and accept the goals.

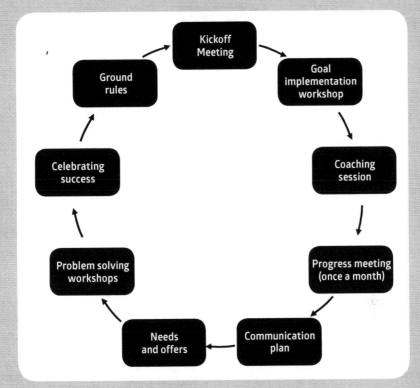

Susanna's annual cycle of leadership.

A few weeks after the kickoff meeting when the team has become familiar with the new goals and has had time to think about their practical meaning, Susanna holds a goal implementation workshop to plan in a concrete way the actions needed to achieve these goals.

Susanna has a coaching session with each team member. Coaching sessions solidify the new goals for each team member right after the goal implementation workshop. As the manager of a team, Susanna feels that the goal implementation workshop and coaching sessions are the most important leadership opportunities for influencing individuals and bringing goals to life.

Susanna also holds a progress meeting once a month. A progress meeting is best for monitoring decisions and actions that have already been agreed upon. Progress meetings check on the results and general atmosphere while the new goals are being implemented. They function as a check-up and provide great opportunities for participants to see the current situation and to align activities. The cornerstone of a progress meeting is active participation, which is needed in order for each participant to commit to action.

On top of all these meetings, she makes a new communication plan to delegate responsibility for stakeholders and holds the needs and offers negotiations every year. In addition, whenever the need arises there are several problem solving workshops or sessions to create new ground rules. At the end of the year she celebrates success and invites the team to a party, which is a virtual party of course. Her virtual party is nothing fancy and it only lasts about an hour. But it is important to bring the team together under purely positive circumstances to celebrate accomplishments and just to chat with each other.

Susanna finds that following an annual cycle of meetings works well for her. But it is important to realize that you cannot become too rigid in following a cycle of meetings; doing so can create problems. If Susanna were think of certain types of meetings belonging to certain parts of the year, she could lose sight of the needs of her team, and the company. The reality is that an annual cycle can be a useful guide to structuring the overall development and leadership program of a team, but a leader always needs to be able to break his or her cycle of meetings if an urgent need arises. Meetings need to be held when a specific problem or situation arises, not just in accordance to an annual meeting cycle. The value in the cycle is to provide a plan on how to systematically lead the team towards its goals.

Susanna is sipping tea with her good facilitator friend George Moose in a pleasant coffee shop in East London. Susanna tells George about her systematic way of organising her meetings in an annual cycle. "Particularly, I am happy about the monthly progress meetings. Progress meetings keep the team focused on goals and we have a lot urgent issues that need attention in our progress meetings," finishes Susanna.

George smiles and praises Susanna. "I am so proud of what you have done. You have a clear system which helps you do this, and most impressive of all, you can do it virtually, too!"

1   Kickoff meeting, Day 1

2   Goal implementation, Day 7

3   Progress meeting, Day 30

4   Progress meeting and Communication plan, Day 60

5   Progress meeting and Offers and needs negotiations, Day 90

6   Progress meeting, Day 120

7   Celebrating success, Day 180

Team performance boost.

George continues, "I use all of the same tools for boosting team performance. The difference between your approach and mine is that I work with the team only for a limited time, around 6 months or so. But I do have the opportunity to use all of the same activities and tools to develop their performance."

"Wow that sounds interesting. Tell me more about it!" says Susanna.

"My clients are global teams that are often not using their full potential. I use this simple model called the *Team performance boost* to help them focus on their goals. First, I agree with the top guy – there are many Bert's in this world – on concrete team goals. Second, I deploy the goals and facilitate a goal implementation workshop for them."

"The teams probably have it difficult swallowing the new goals created by the Berts?"

"Sure they do. Nevertheless, the kickoff meeting and goal implementation workshop help them to deal with negative emotions, understand the goals and to create an agreement on how to take the changes forward. The teams are seldom focused, and I see how this one activity focusing people on goals and aligning activities makes a huge difference."

"Very, very interesting. Our management team has a new strategy that they agreed upon together, but the guys are missing all deadlines and not even answering each other's calls or emails. Do you have any ideas about what to do with them?" Susanna asked her friend.

"It seems that they have an understanding on goals, but they have not agreed on the way of working. You could try to facilitate a virtual progress meeting for those guys. First you see what is going well with the strategy and next you write all current challenges on the whiteboard. Finally, you let them suggest solutions for their challenges. They should be clever enough to at least think of some solutions on how to keep connected. Progress meeting are a key element to leading and supporting high performance."

George gets excited about the topic and continues chatting away. "And I use all the other team activities as well! My teams have problem solving meetings, they create communication plans, I hold coaching sessions for the managers and I facilitate needs and offers negotiations. There was this global IT team that was having real trust issues. The success of the team depended on international co-operation but actually the French, Germans and Americans were only working within their own national groups. I forced the team members to connect with 'outsiders' by using the needs and offers negotiations. They were put into pairs and forced to talk to people outside of their clique. Once they did this they realised what the others could offer them, and what they could offer in return."

"George, that sound like a good idea. Do you ever meet teams without any problems?"

"Sure, I do. There are many high performing teams that work well and are even accustomed to solving their own challenges. But interestingly enough, all teams get tired at some point. These teams need to renew themselves constantly in order to stay effective."

"And I suppose you have a tool for that too, right?"

"You start a new performance boost. You create new challenging goals for them, develop their ways of working, or give them a better view of the market and internal challenges with a problem solving workshop. Anything that shakes things up a little bit and brings the team outside of their normal routine will work just fine."

"Thank you, George. That was a nice introduction on how to use different tools for boosting team performance. But be careful. At the rate I am learning, you may have some new competition in the business consulting field," Susanna exclaims.

LOOKING BACK AND FORWARD

Susanna looks back on her journey in world of leadership. She has learned so much about how to apply basic leadership tools to face-to-face and virtual working environments, and the technology required doesn't seem to be any sort of limitation.

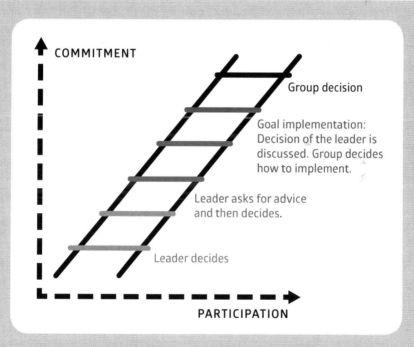

Participation creates commitment.

During her journey Susanna experienced first-hand the benefits of Facilitative leadership. No one likes being bossed around, even if it is a part of your job. Facilitative leadership eliminates this. First, participation in decision making increases commitment and employee motivation. Second, it increases creativity and innovation. When employees are given the chance to discuss important things together, new innovations and ways of working are born. And lastly, workshops help people co-ordinate their tasks and daily working activities better which results in higher achieving teams.

Susanna feels that she is on the right track, and that her new facilitative leadership style is working. But can she be sure?

The leadership cycle is not easy, it requires quite a lot of work and organising and Susanna wonders if she managed to pull it off. As she frequently does in moments of doubt, Susanna calls George.

"Remember our chat about lions killing tigers?"

George laughs, and he is delighted to hear from Susanna. "Of course, I do. It was an important conversation if I remember correctly."

"You're right, it was important...even though I didn't realize it at the time. I'm calling to ask you a bit of a strange question. I have tried my best to lead like a lion; be balanced, create alignment, and lead a decisive group, and I think I pulled it off."

"I'm sure of it too, Susanna."

"I see the results; the team is more focused and independent. Also, we get far better financial results. But...the team members are arguing with me and they seem to have far more conflict with each other, too. Am I really doing everything right?"

George smiles; he can relate to Susanna's moment of personal doubt.

"Let me tell you one more thing about lions, Susanna. They are always confident. Can you imagine a lion acting timid or unsure?"

Besides the lion in the Wizard of Oz, Susanna could not.

"Susanna, I'm not saying that you shouldn't reflect on your performance as a leader. In fact, it is good that you are questioning yourself a bit. You have empowered your team and now the team members feel confident on what they are doing. Before your team members had to come and ask you for guidance, now they know where to go and what to do. Confident and empowered people try their limits and borders. It is the negative side of democracy and the reason why many people are afraid of empowerment. But what I am trying to say is that even if the lions are sometimes fighting with each other, the lions have a plan and they work together. It leads them to success."

"George, is there anything I can do to tame my lions?"

"Of course there is. You could help them create ground rules for working with each other. But empowered team members always tend to be more conflictual than people working in a hierarchy since they believe they have the right to realise their own ideas. People have lots of ideas and sometimes they are conflicting. That is just a fact of life."

Susanna caught on. "And I have my plan, I just return back to my team performance boost and trust my team..."

George was happy; hearing Susanna reflect on her doubts and then realize that she had the tools in front of her to resolve those doubts and strengthen her leadership showed George that Susanna was indeed a good student, and a promising facilitative leader.

GUIDELINES FOR USING VIRTUAL PLATFORMS

SKYPE FOR BUSINESS QUICK GUIDE

Jonas Lindström / 31.10.2017 / © Grape People Finland

Skype for Business is developed as a service and gets occasional user interface updates. This means your client may display some menus slightly differently from this guide.

The screenshots in this guide have been taken with Skype for Business 2016 version 16.0.7927.1020 and the Skype for Business web client as of May 5th, 2017.

Skype for Business will be abbreviated as "Skype" in this guide from now on.

STARTING A SKYPE MEETING

Skype invitation

From Outlook
Calendar choose
**New Skype
Meeting**

Outlook
automatically
generates a "Join
Skype meeting"
link into the
invitation,
and meeting
participants can
join by clicking this link.

Note that Skype must be open & signed in for this feature to work.

Choosing Skype audio

When entering the
Skype meeting,
from the **Join
Meeting Audio**
window choose **Use
Skype for Business
(full audio and
video experience)**.

Skype online meeting symbols

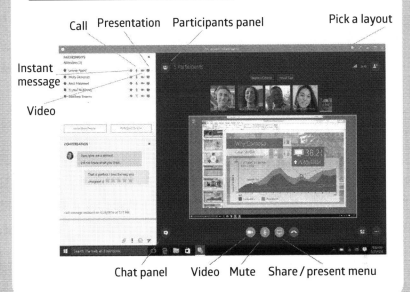

Choosing Skype layout

Depending on your meeting type, you can select a specific view of **content, speaker,** or **gallery** by using the 🔲 Pick a layout button.

- **Gallery View** shows all the participants' pictures or videos
- **Speaker View** shows the meeting content with the presenter's video or picture in the lower-right corner of the meeting window
- **Content** or **Presentation View** shows only the meeting content. *We recommend using this view so the participants can fully focus on the meeting content.*

MANAGING MEETING AND PRESENTING PERMISSIONS

Setting permissions before meeting

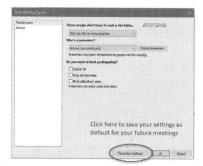

From the Outlook calendar event you can change the Meeting Options.

These are good default settings for internal meetings – but I usually restrict settings a bit more if the group is large and / or the participants are not adept at using Skype. (See next 2 slides)

Setting permissions in-meeting

Three dot menu

Skype Meeting Options

Here you can control presenting permissions. (Recommended settings next page)

Recommended meeting permissions

Recommended settings for internal meetings or when everyone is adept at using Skype

Recommended settings for large / external meetings / when everyone is not adept at using Skype

SHARING IN SKYPE

Sharing in Skype

You can share (Present) content in Skype:

- **Desktop** – shares your entire desktop
- **Window** – share a single window
- **PowerPoint** – share a ppt file*
- **More** → **Whiteboard** – create new whiteboard*
- **More** → **Poll** – create new Poll

*meeting participants can make annotations (i.e draw, write, stamp etc.)

Polling – how to?

Polling is easy:

1. Go to **Share** menu – choose **More** → **Poll**.
2. Fill in the question and choices.
   When ready click **Create** and the poll is opened.

Sharing a whiteboard – how to?

Creating a new whiteboard:

1. Go to **Present** menu – choose **Whiteboard**
2. Write, draw, stamp and point on the whiteboard

Sharing a ppt – how to?

Sharing a ppt:

1. Go to Present menu – choose PowerPoint

2. Annotations – tool set icon on the upper-right side of the PowerPoint

Manage presentable content

You can navigate the shared content within the **Manage Content** window.

IN CASE YOU LOSE YOUR WAY...(A.K.A. PRIVATE VIEW)

Private view

You can privately view presentation content and return to **Presenter's View** whenever you like

Take Over as a Presenter when you want to present to all meeting participants

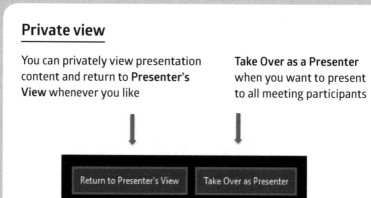

N.B. that these buttons are *only* visible when a) someone else is presenting b) you have private viewing permissions c) you are viewing content privately (e.g. changing slides on your own)

HOW TO USE BREAKOUT SESSIONS

Creating additional meetings for breakout sessions

· **How many meetings will you need?** The number of meetings depends on the amount of participants and discussion topics. 2–4 people per meeting is a good target. If there are lots of participants, 5 person groups are OK too.

· **Create the meetings in your calendar.** These are normal Skype meetings, just like the main event.

· Copy the meeting links into a notepad

→

- Paste the meeting links into the **chat** when you want people to move into the breakout rooms

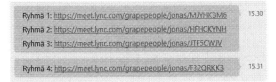

Ryhmä 1: https://meet.lync.com/grapepeople/jonas/MJYHK3M6   15.30
Ryhmä 2: https://meet.lync.com/grapepeople/jonas/HFHCKYNH
Ryhmä 3: https://meet.lync.com/grapepeople/jonas/JTF5CWJV

Ryhmä 4: https://meet.lync.com/grapepeople/jonas/F32QRKK3   15.31

- **Alternative**: Delegate the creation of meetings to the participants. Assign a facilitator to each group and let him/her create the meeting and invite the others.

Breakout session instructions

1. Give written instructions

2. Repeat the **topic(s)** of the breakout sessions

3. Ask participants to **register** for the groups (/topics) according to their interest

4. The so-called **rush method** means that each group has a max number of participants, after which it is full.

5. Assign a **facilitator / scribe** for each group

6. Give the groups a **time slot** for working and mark the **return time** on the slide

7. Give the groups a **go signal**

Breakout groups	Participants
Group 1 (Topic 1)	
Group 2 (Topic 2)	
Group 3 (Topic 3)	
Group 4 (Topic 4)	

KEY WEBEX TRAINING CENTER FUNCTIONS FOR INTERACTIVE MEETINGS

© Grape People Finland

Steps to set up break out sessions

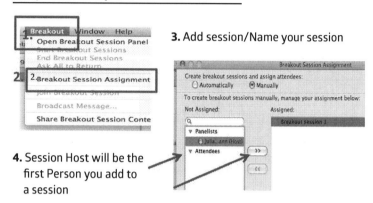

3. Add session/Name your session

4. Session Host will be the first Person you add to a session

5. Then Add attendees to each session (attendees are transferred to the session which is marked and dark blue)

Participant rights

Make sure everyone can annotate powerpoints and whiteboard:
Assign privileges

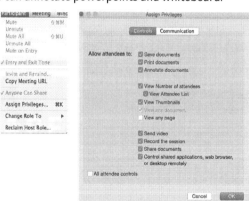

Drawing and Writing

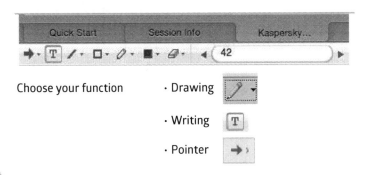

Choose your function
- Drawing
- Writing [T]
- Pointer →›

Mute

- Mute when necessary

Help!

Raise your hand, if you are here (or in trouble)

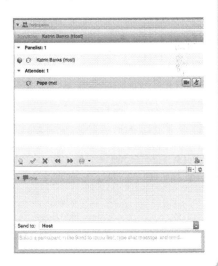

Whiteboard

Open a whiteboard by clicking

Saving the whiteboard content

When leaving the session presenter saves the whiteboard.

Choose: File and Save

A pop-up window appears. Save the file on your desk-top.

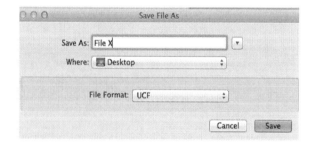

Controlling the slide show

1. Change to next or previous slide

2. Synchronize your view with the presenters view

3. Adapt the size of the slide show here

Sharing powerpoints

Upload powerpoints by clicking Share and File. If you share your desktop, the Participants can not write on your powerpoints

Set up a Poll

1. Open Poll Panel

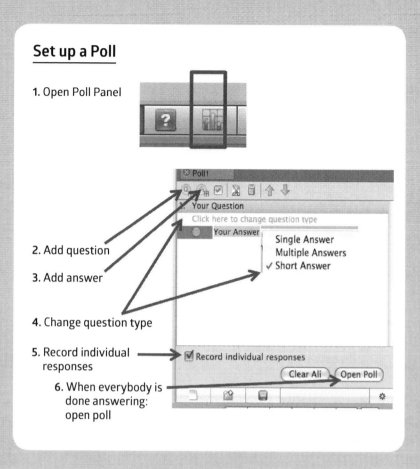

2. Add question

3. Add answer

4. Change question type

5. Record individual responses

    6. When everybody is done answering: open poll

Made in the USA
Middletown, DE
12 August 2020